The Constitution of
The State of Ohio:
A Quick Reference Guide

Bootblack Budget Books
Copyright 2018 ©
ISBN-13: 978-1720481348
ISBN-10: 1720481342

Contents:

Preamble – Page 30

Article I: Bill of Rights – Page 31

Section 1. Inalienable Rights

Section 2. Right to Alter, Reform, or Abolish Government, and Repeal Special Privileges

Section 3. Right to Assemble

Section 4. Bearing Arms; Standing Armies; Military Power

Section 5. Trial by Jury

Section 6. Slavery and Involuntary Servitude

Section 7. Rights of Conscience; Education; the Necessity of Religion and Knowledge

Section 8. Writ of Habeas Corpus

Section 9. Bail

Section 10. Trial for Crimes; Witness

Section 10a. Rights of Victims of Crime

Section 11. Freedom of Speech; of the Press; of Libels

Section 12. Transportation, Etc. for Crime

Section 13. Quartering Troops

Section 14. Search Warrants and General Warrants

Section 15. No Imprisonment for Debt

Section 16. Redress for Injury; Due Process

Section 17. No Hereditary Privileges

Section 18. Suspension of Laws

Section 19. Eminent Domain

Section 19a. Damages for Wrongful Death

Section 19b. Protect Private Property Rights in Ground Water, Lakes and Other Watercourses

Section 20. Powers Reserved to the People

Article II: Legislative – Page 40

Section 1. In Whom Power Vested

Section 1a. Initiative and Referendum to Amend Constitution

Section 1b. Initiative and Referendum to Enact Laws

Section 1c. Referendum to Challenge Laws Enacted by General Assembly

Section 1d. Emergency Laws; Not Subject to Referendum

Section 1e. Powers; Limitation of Use

Section 1f. Power of Municipalities

Section 1g. Petition Requirements and Preparation; Submission; Ballot Language; by Ohio Ballot Board

Section 2. Election and Term of State Legislators

Section 3. Residence Requirements for State Legislators

Section 4. Dual Office and Conflict of Interest Prohibited

Section 5. Who Shall Not Hold Office

Section 6. Powers of Each House

Section 7. Organization of Each House of the General Assembly

Section 8. Sessions of the General Assembly

Section 9. House and Senate Journals (Yeas and Nays)

Section 10. Rights of Members to Protest

Section 11. Filling Vacancy in House or Senate Seat

Section 12. Privilege of Members from Arrest and of Speech

Section 13. Legislative Sessions to Be Public; Exceptions

Section 14. Power of Adjournment

Section 15. How Bills Shall be Passed

Section 16. Bills to Be Signed by Governor; Veto

Section 17. Repealed

Section 18. Repealed

Section 19. Repealed

Section 20. Term of Office, and Compensation of Officers in Certain Cases

Section 21. Contested Elections

Section 22. Appropriations

Section 23. Impeachments; How Instituted and Conducted

Section 24. Officers Liable to Impeachment; Consequences

Section 25. Repealed

Section 26. Laws to Have a Uniform Operation

Section 27. Election and Appointment of Officers; Filling Vacancies

Section 28. Retroactive Laws

Section 29. No Extra Compensation; Exceptions

Section 30. New Counties

Section 31. Compensation of Members and Officers of the General Assembly

Section 32. Divorces and Judicial Power

Section 33. Mechanics' and Contractor's Liens

Section 34. Welfare of Employees

Section 34a. Minimum Wage

Section 35. Workers' Compensation

Section 36. Conservation of Natural Resources

Section 37. Workday and Workweek on Public Projects

Section 38. Removal of Officials for Misconduct

Section 39. Regulating Expert Testimony in Criminal Trials

Section 40. Registering and Warranting Land Titles

Section 41. Prison Labor

Section 42. Continuity of Government Operations in Emergencies Caused by Enemy Attack

Article III: Executive – Page 65

Section 1. Executive Department; Key State Officers

Section 1a. Joint Vote Cast for Governor and Lieutenant

Section 1b. Lieutenant Governor Duties Assigned by Governor

Section 2. Term of Office of Key State Officers

Section 3. Counting Votes for Key State Officers

Section 4. Repealed

Section 5. Executive Power Vested in Governor

Section 6. Governor to See that Laws Executed; May Require Written Information

Section 7. Governor's Annual Message to General Assembly; Recommendations for Legislation

Section 8. Governor May Convene Special Session of Legislature with Limited Purposes

Section 9. When Governor May Adjourn the Legislature

Section 10. Governor is Commander-in-Chief of Militia

Section 11. Governor May Grant Reprieves, Commutations and Pardons

Section 12. Seal of the State, and by Whom Kept

Section 13. How Grants and Commissions Issued

Section 14. Who is Ineligible for Governor

Section 15. Succession in Case of Vacancy in Office of Governor

Section 16. Repealed

Section 17. If a Vacancy Shall Occur While Executing the Office of Governor, Who Shall Act

Section 17a. Filling a Vacancy in the Office of Lieutenant Governor

Section 18. Governor to Fill Vacancies in Key State Offices

Section 19. Compensation of Key State Officers

Section 20. Annual Report of Executive Officers

Section 21. Appointments to Office; Advice and Consent of Senate

Section 22. Supreme Court to Determine Disability of Governor or Governor Elect; Succession

Article IV: Judicial – Page 74

Section 1. Judicial Power Vested in Court

Section 2. Organization and Jurisdiction of Supreme Court

Section 3: Organization and Jurisdiction of Court of Appeals

Section 4. Organization and Jurisdiction of Common Pleas Court

Section 5. Powers and Duties of Supreme Court; Rules

Section 6. Election of Judges; Compensation

Section 7. Repealed

Section 8. Repealed

Section 9. Repealed

Section 10. Repealed

Section 11. Repealed

Section 12. Repealed

Section 13. Vacancy in Office of Judge, How Filled

Section 14. Repealed

Section 15. Changing Number of Judges; Establishing Other Courts

Section 16. Repealed

Section 17. Judges Removable

Section 18. Powers and Jurisdiction of Judges

Section 19. Courts of Conciliation

Section 20. Style of Process, Prosecution, and Indictment

Section 21/22. Supreme Court Commission

Section 23. Judges in Less Populous Counties; Service on More than One Court

Article V: Elective Franchise – Page 85

Section 1. Who May Vote

Section 2. By Ballot

Section 2a. Names of Candidates on Ballot

Section 3. Repealed

Section 4. Exclusion from Franchise

Section 5. Repealed

Section 6. Idiots or Insane Persons

Section 7. Primary Elections

Section 8. Term Limits for U.S. Senators and Representatives

Section 9. Eligibility of Officeholders

Article VI: Education – Page 88

Section 1. Funds for Religious and Educational Purposes

Section 2. School Funds

Section 3. Public School System, Boards of Education

Section 4. State Board of Education

Section 5. Loans for Higher Education

Section 6. Tuition Credits Program

Article VII: Public Institutions – Page 91

Section 1. Inane, Blind, and Deaf and Dumb

Section 2. Directors of Penitentiary, Trustees of Benevolent and Other State Institutions; How Appointed

Section 3. Filling Vacancies in Directorships of State Institutions

Article VIII: Public Debt and Public Works – Page 92

Section 1. Public Debt; Limit of Deficit Spending by State

Section 2. State May Incur Debts for Defense or to Retire Outstanding Debts

Section 2a. Repealed

Section 2b. Adjusted Compensation for Service in World War II; World War II Veterans' Bonuses

Section 2c. Construction of State Highway System

Section 2d. Korean War Veterans' Bonuses

Section 2e. Providing Means for Securing Funds for Highway and Public Building Construction

Section 2f. Authorizing Bond Issue to Provide School Classrooms, Support for Universities, for Recreation and Conservation and for State Buildings

Section 2g. Authorizing Bond Issue or Other Obligations for Highway Construction

Section 2h. Bond Issue for State Development

Section 2i. Capital Improvement Bonds

Section 2j. Vietnam Conflict Compensation Fund

Section 2k. Issuance of Bonds for Local Government Public Infrastructure Capital Improvements

Section 2l. Parks, Recreation, and Natural Resources Project Capital Improvements

Section 2m. Issuance of General Obligations

Section 2n. Facilities for System of Common Schools and Facilities for State-Supported and State-Assisted Institutions of Higher Education

Section 2o. Issuance of Bonds and Other Obligations for Environmental Conservation and Revitalization Purposes

Section 2p. Issuance of Bonds for Economic and Educational Purposes and Local Government Projects

Section 2q. Issuance of Bonds for Continuation of Environmental Revitalization and Conservation

Section 2r. Issue bonds to provide compensation to veterans of the Persian Gulf, Afghanistan, and Iraq conflicts

Section 2s.

Section 3. The State to Create No Other Debt; Exceptions

Section 4. Credit of State; the State Shall Not Become Joint Owner or Stockholder

Section 5. No Assumption of Debts by the State

Section 6. Countries, Cities, Towns, or Townships, Not Authorized to Become Stockholders, Etc.; Insurance, Etc.

Section 7. Sinking Fund

Section 8. The Commissioners of the Sinking Fund

Section 9. Biennial Report of Sinking Fund Commissioners

Section 10. Application of Sinking Fund

Section 11. Semiannual Report of Sinking Fund Commissioners

Section 12. Repealed

Section 13. Economic Development

Section 14. Financing for Housing Program

Section 15. State Assistance to Development of Coal Technology

Section 16. State and Political Subdivisions to Provide Housing for Individuals

Section 17. Limitations on Obligations State May Issue

Article IX: Militia – Page 173

Section 1. Who Shall Perform Military Duty

Section 2. Repealed

Section 3. Appointment of Militia Officers

Section 4. Power of Governor to Call Forth Militia

Section 5. Public Arms; Arsenals

Article X: **County and Township Organizations** – Page 174

Section 1. Organization and Government of Counties; County Home Rule; Submission

Section 2. Township Officers; Election; Power

Section 3. County Charters; Approval by Voters

Section 4. County Charter Commission; Election, Etc.

Section 5. Repealed

Section 6. Repealed

Section 7. Repealed

Article XI: Apportionment – Page 179
(Sections Are Not Titled)

Section 1.

Section 2.

Section 3.

Section 4.

Section 5.

Section 6.

Section 7.

Section 8.

Section 9.

Section 10.

Article XII: Finance and Taxation – Page 192

Section 1. Poll Taxes Prohibited

Section 2. Limitation on Tax Rate; Exemption

Section 2a. Authority to Classify Real Estate for Taxation; Procedures

Section 3. Imposition of Taxes

Section 4. Revenue to Pay Expenses and Retire Debts

Section 5. Levying of Taxes

Section 5a. Use of Motor Vehicle License and Fuel Taxes Restricted

Section 6. No Debt for Internal Improvement

Section 7. Repealed

Section 8. Repealed

Section 9. Apportionment of Income, Estate, and Inheritance Taxes

Section 10. Repealed

Section 11. Sinking Fund

Section 12. Repealed

Section 13. Wholesale Taxes on Foods

Article XIII: Corporations – Page 198

Section 1. Special Acts Conferring Corporate Powers; Prohibited

Section 2. Corporations, How Formed

Section 3. Liability of Stockholders for Unpaid Subscriptions; Dues from Corporations; How Secured; Inspection of Private Banks

Section 4. Corporate Property Subject to Taxation

Section 5. Corporate Power to Eminent Domain to Obtain Rights of Way; Procedure; Jury Trial

Section 6. Organization of Cities, Etc.

Section 7. Acts Authorizing Associations with Banking Powers; Referendum

Article XIV: Agriculture – Page 200

Section 1. Ohio Livestock Care Standards Board

Article XV: Miscellaneous – Page 202

Section 1. Seat of Government

Section 2. Repealed

Section 3. Receipts and Expenditures; Publication of State Financial Statements

Section 4. Officers to Be Qualified Electors

Section 5. Repealed

Section 6. Lotteries, Charitable Bingo

Section 7. Oath of Officers

Section 8. Repealed

Section 9. Repealed

Section 9a. Repealed

Section 10. Civil Service

Section 11. Marriage

Article XVI: Amendments – Page 212

Section 1. How Constitution to Be Amended; Ballot; Supreme Court to Hear Challenges

Section 2. Convention

Section 3. Question of Constitutional Convention to Be Submitted Periodically

Article XVII: Elections – Page 215

Section 1. Time for Holding

Section 2. Terms of Officers, Vacancies, Etc

Section 3. Repealed

Article XVIII: Municipal Corporations – Page 217

Section 1. Classification

Section 2. General and Additional Laws

Section 3. Powers

Section 4. Acquisition of Public Utility; Contract for Service; Condemnation

Section 5. Acquisition by Ordinance; Procedure; Referendum; Submission

Section 6. Sale of Surplus

Section 7. Home Rule

Section 8. Submission of Question of Election of Charter Commission; Approval

Section 9. Amendments to Charter; Submission; Approval

Section 10. Appropriation in Excess of Public Use

Section 11. Assessments for Cost of Appropriating Property

Section 12. Bonds for Public Utilities

Section 13. Taxation, Debts, Reports, and Accounts

Section 14. Elections

Article XIX: Congressional Redistricting – Page 222
(Sections Have No Titles)

Section 1.

Section 2.

Section 3.

Schedule – Page 231

Section 1. Of Prior Laws

Section 2. The First Election of Members of General Assembly

Section 3. For State Officers

Section 4. For Judges, Clerks, Etc

Section 5. Officers to Continue in Office until the Expiration of Their Terms

Section 6. Certain Courts

Section 7. County and Township Officers

Section 8. Vacancies

Section 9. When Constitution Shall Take Effect

Section 10. Term of Office

Section 11. Transfer of Suits, Supreme Court

Section 12. Transfer of Suits, District Courts

Section 13. Transfer of Suits, Courts of Common Pleas

Section 14. Transfer of Suits, Probate Courts

Section 15. Judges and Clerks, How Elected, Etc

Section 16. Election Returns, When Sent

Section 17. Constitution Submitted to the Electors of the State

Section 18. License to Traffic in Intoxicating Liquors

Section 19. Apportionment for House of Representatives

Section 20. General schedule

Section 20a. Method of Submission

Section 21. Schedule to Article 2 Sections 1, 1a, 1b, 1c, 1d, 1e, 1f, and 1g

Section 22. Schedule to Article 4 Sections 1, 2, 3, 6, 7, 12, and 15

Section 23. Schedule to Article 6 Sections 3 and 4

Section 24. Schedule to Article 18 Sections 1-14

Section 25. Schedule to Article 15 Section 9

Section 26. Schedule to Article 12 Sections 2 and 3

Section 27. Schedule to Article 12 Sections 2 and 3

Section 28. Schedule to Article 12 Section 2

Section 29. Schedule to Article 6 Section 4

Section 30. Schedule to Article 4 Sections 1-14 and Article 11 Sections 12 and 13

Section 31. Schedule to Article 3 Sections 1b and 16

Section 32. Schedule to Article 3 Section 22

Section 33. Schedule to Article 12 Section 9

Preamble

We, the people of the State of Ohio, grateful to Almighty God for our freedom, to secure its blessings and promote our common welfare, do establish this Constitution.

ARTICLE I: BILL OF RIGHTS

Section 1. Inalienable Rights

All men are, by nature, free and independent, and have certain inalienable rights, among which are those of enjoying and defending life and liberty, acquiring, possessing, and protecting property, and seeking and obtaining happiness and safety.

Section 2. Right to Alter, Reform, or Abolish Government, and Repeal Special Privileges

All political power is inherent in the people. Government is instituted for their equal protection and benefit, and they have the right to alter, reform, or abolish the same, whenever they may deem it necessary; and no special privileges or immunities shall ever be granted, that may not be altered, revoked, or repealed by the General Assembly.

Section 3. Right to Assemble

The people have the right to assemble together, in a peaceable manner, to consult for the common good; to instruct their representatives; and to petition the General Assembly for the redress of grievances.

Section 4. Bearing Arms; Standing Armies; Military Power

The people have the right to bear arms for their defense and security; but standing armies, in time of peace, are dangerous to liberty, and shall not be kept up; and the military shall be in strict subordination to the civil power.

Section 5. Trial by Jury

The right of trial by jury shall be inviolate, except that, in civil cases, laws may be passed to authorize the rendering of a verdict by the concurrence of not less than three-fourths of the jury.

Section 6. Slavery and Involuntary Servitude

There shall be no slavery in this state; nor involuntary servitude, unless for the punishment of crime.

Section 7. Rights of Conscience; Education; the Necessity of Religion and Knowledge

All men have a natural and indefeasible right to worship Almighty God according to the dictates of their own conscience. No person shall be compelled to attend, erect, or support any place of worship, or maintain any form of worship, against his consent; and no preference shall be given, by law, to any religious society; nor shall any interference with the rights of conscience be permitted. No religious test shall be required, as a qualification for office, nor shall any person be incompetent to be a witness on account of his religious belief; but nothing herein shall be construed to dispense with oaths and affirmations. Religion, morality, and knowledge, however, being essential to good government, it shall be the duty of the General Assembly to pass suitable laws, to protect every religious denomination in the peaceable enjoyment of its own mode of public worship, and to encourage schools and the means of instruction.

Section 8. Writ of Habeas Corpus

The privilege of the writ of habeas corpus shall not be suspended, unless, in cases of rebellion or invasion, the public safety require it.

Section 9. Bail

All persons shall be bailable by sufficient sureties, except for a person who is charged with a capital offense where the proof is evident or the presumption great and except for a person who is charged with a felony where the proof is evident or the presumption great and who where the person poses a substantial risk of serious physical harm to any person or to the community. Where a person is charged with any offense for which the person may be incarcerated, the court may determine at any time the type, amount, and conditions of bail. Excessive bail shall not be required; nor excessive fines imposed; nor cruel and unusual punishments inflicted. The General Assembly shall fix by law standards to determine whether a person who is charged with a felony where the proof is evident or the presumption great poses a substantial risk of serious physical harm to any person or to the community. Procedures for establishing the amount and conditions of bail shall be established pursuant to Article IV, Section 5(b) of the Constitution of the State of Ohio.

Section 10. Trial for Crimes; Witness

Except in cases of impeachment, cases arising in the army and navy, or in the militia when in actual service in time of war or public danger, and cases involving offenses for which the penalty provided is less than imprisonment in the penitentiary, no person shall be held to answer for a capital, or otherwise infamous, crime, unless on presentment or indictment of a grand jury; and the number of persons necessary to constitute such grand jury and the number thereof necessary to concur in finding such indictment shall be determined by law. In any trial, in any court, the party accused shall be allowed to appear and defend in person and with counsel; to demand the nature and cause of the accusation against him, and to have a copy thereof; to meet witnesses face to face, and to have compulsory process to procure the attendance of witnesses in his behalf, and speedy public trial by an impartial jury of the county in which the offense is alleged to have been committed; but provision may be made by law for the taking of the deposition by the accused or by the state, to be used for or against the accused, of any witness whose attendance can not be had at the trial, always securing to the accused means and the opportunity to be present in person and with counsel at the taking of such deposition, and to examine the witness face to face as fully and in the same manner as if in court. No person shall be compelled, in any criminal case, to be a witness against himself; but his failure to testify may be considered by the court and jury and may be the subject of comment by counsel. No person shall be twice put in jeopardy for the same offense.

Section 10a. Rights of Victims of Crime

(A) To secure for victims justice and due process throughout the criminal and juvenile justice systems, a victim shall have the following rights, which shall be protected in a manner no less vigorous than the rights afforded to the accused:

(1) to be treated with fairness and respect for the victim's safety, dignity and privacy;

(2) upon request, to reasonable and timely notice of all public proceedings involving the criminal offense or delinquent act against the victim, and to be present at all such proceedings;

(3) to be heard in any public proceeding involving release, plea, sentencing, disposition, or parole, or in any public proceeding in which a right of the victim is implicated;

(4) to reasonable protection from the accused or any person acting on behalf of the accused;

(5) upon request, to reasonable notice of any release or escape of the accused;

(6) except as authorized by section 10 of Article I of this constitution, to refuse an interview, deposition, or other discovery request made by the accused or any person acting on behalf of the accused;

(7) to full and timely restitution from the person who committed the criminal offense or delinquent act against the victim;

(8) to proceedings free from unreasonable delay and a prompt conclusion of the case;

(9) upon request, to confer with the attorney for the government; and

(10) to be informed, in writing, of all rights enumerated in this section.

(B) The victim, the attorney for the government upon request of the victim, or the victim's other lawful representative, in any proceeding involving the criminal offense or delinquent act against the victim or in which the victim's rights are implicated, may assert the rights enumerated in this section and any other right afforded to the victim by law. If the relief sought is denied, the victim or the victim's lawful representative may petition the court of appeals for the applicable district, which shall promptly consider and decide the petition.

(C) This section does not create any cause of action for damages or compensation against the state, any political subdivision of the state, any officer, employee, or agent of the state or of any political subdivision, or any officer of the court.

(D) As used in this section, "victim" means a person against whom the criminal offense or delinquent act is committed or who is directly and proximately harmed by the commission of the offense or act. The term "victim" does not include the accused or a person whom the court finds would not act in the best interests of a deceased, incompetent, minor, or incapacitated victim.

(E) All provisions of this section shall be self-executing and severable, and shall supersede all conflicting state laws.

(F) This section shall take effect ninety days after the election at which it was approved.

Section 11. Freedom of Speech; of the Press; of Libels

Every citizen may freely speak, write, and publish his sentiments on all subjects, being responsible for the abuse of the right; and no law shall be passed to restrain or abridge the liberty of speech, or of the press. In all criminal prosecutions for libel, the truth may be given in evidence to the jury, and if it shall appear to the jury, that the matter charged as libelous is true, and was published with good motives, and for justifiable ends, the party shall be acquitted.

Section 12. Transportation, Etc. for Crime

No person shall be transported out of the state, for any offense committed within the same; and no conviction shall work corruption of blood, or forfeiture of estate.

Section 13. Quartering Troops

No soldier shall, in time of peace, be quartered in any house, without the consent of the owner; nor, in time of war, except in the manner prescribed by law.

Section 14. Search Warrants and General Warrants

The right of the people to be secure in their persons, houses, papers, and possessions, against unreasonable searches and seizures shall not be violated; and no warrant shall issue, but upon probable cause, supported by oath or affirmation, particularly describing the place to be searched and the person and things to be seized.

Section 15. No Imprisonment for Debt

No person shall be imprisoned for debt in any civil action, on mesne or final process, unless in cases of fraud.

Section 16. Redress for Injury; Due Process

All courts shall be open, and every person, for an injury done him in his land, goods, person, or reputation, shall have remedy by due course of law, and shall have justice administered without denial or delay. Suits may be brought against the state, in such courts and in such manner, as may be provided by law.

Section 17. No Hereditary Privileges

No hereditary emoluments, honors, or privileges, shall ever be granted or conferred by this State.

Section 18. Suspension of Laws

No power of suspending laws shall ever be exercised, except by the General Assembly.

Section 19. Eminent Domain

Private property shall ever be held inviolate, but subservient to the public welfare. When taken in time of war or other public exigency, imperatively requiring its immediate seizure or for the purpose of making or repairing roads, which shall be open to the public, without charge, a compensation shall be made to the owner, in money, and in all other cases, where private property shall be taken for public use, a compensation therefore shall first be made in money, or first secured by a deposit of money; and such compensation shall be assessed by a jury, without deduction for benefits to any property of the owner.

Section 19a. Damages for Wrongful Death
The amount of damages recoverable by civil action in the courts

for death caused by the wrongful act, neglect, or default of another, shall not be limited by law.

Section 19b. Protect Private Property Rights in Ground Water, Lakes and Other Watercourses

(A) The protection of the rights of Ohio's property owners, the protection of Ohio's natural resources, and the maintenance of the stability of Ohio's economy require the recognition and protection of property interests in ground water, lakes, and watercourses.

(B) The preservation of private property interests recognized under divisions (C) and (D) of this section shall be held inviolate, but subservient to the public welfare as provided in Section 19 of Article I of the Constitution.

(C) A property owner has a property interest in the reasonable use of the ground water underlying the property owner's land.

(D) An owner of riparian land has a property interest in the reasonable use of the water in a lake or watercourse located on or flowing through the owner's riparian land.

(E) Ground water underlying privately owned land and nonnavigable waters located on or flowing through privately owned land shall not be held in trust by any governmental body. The state, and a political subdivision to the extent authorized by state law, may provide for the regulation of such waters. An owner of land voluntarily may convey to a governmental body the owner's property interest held in the ground water underlying the land or nonnavigable waters located on or flowing through the land.

(F) Nothing in this section affects the application of the public trust doctrine as it applies to Lake Erie or the navigable waters of the state.

(G) Nothing in Section 1e of Article II, Section 36 of Article II, Article VIII, Section 1 of Article X, Section 3 of Article XVIII, or Section 7 of Article XVIII of the Constitution shall impair or limit the rights established in this section.

Section 20. Powers Reserved to the People

This enumeration of rights shall not be construed to impair or deny others retained by the people, and all powers, not herein delegated, remain with the people.

ARTICLE II: LEGISLATURE

Section 1. In Whom Power Vested

The legislative power of the state shall be vested in a General Assembly consisting of a Senate and House of Representatives but the people reserve to themselves the power to propose to the General Assembly laws and amendments to the constitution, and to adopt or reject the same at the polls on a referendum vote as hereinafter provided. They also reserve the power to adopt or reject any law, section of any law or any item in any law appropriating money passed by the General Assembly, except as herein after provided; and independent of the General Assembly to propose amendments to the constitution and to adopt or reject the same at the polls. The limitations expressed in the constitution, on the power of the General Assembly to enact laws, shall be deemed limitations on the power of the people to enact laws.

Section 1a. Initiative and Referendum to Amend Constitution

The first aforestated power reserved by the people is designated the initiative, and the signatures of ten per centum of the electors shall be required upon a petition to propose an amendment to the constitution. When a petition signed by the aforesaid required number of electors, shall have been filed with the secretary of state, and verified as herein provided, proposing an amendment to the constitution, the full text of which shall have been set forth in such petition, the secretary of state shall submit for the approval or rejection of the electors, the proposed amendment, in the manner hereinafter provided, at the next succeeding regular or general election in any year occurring subsequent to one hundred twenty-five days after the filing of such petition. The initiative petitions, above described, shall have printed across the top thereof: "Amendment to the Constitution Proposed by Initiative Petition to be Submitted Directly to the Electors."

Section 1b. Initiative and Referendum to Enact Laws

When at any time, not less than ten days prior to the commencement of any session of the General Assembly, there shall have been filed with the secretary of state a petition signed by three per centum of the electors and verified as herein provided, proposing a law, the full text of which shall have been set forth in such petition, the secretary of state shall transmit the same to the General Assembly as soon as it convenes. If said proposed law shall be passed by the General Assembly, either as petitioned for or in an amended form, it shall be subject to the referendum. If it shall not be passed, or if it shall be passed in an amended form, or if no action shall be taken thereon within four months from the time it is received by the General Assembly, it shall be submitted by the secretary of state to the electors for their approval or rejection, if such submission shall be demanded by supplementary petition verified as herein provided and signed by not less than three per centum of the electors in addition to those signing the original petition, which supplementary petition must be signed and filed with the secretary of state within ninety days after the proposed law shall have been rejected by the General Assembly or after the expiration of such term of four months, if no action has been taken thereon, or after the law as passed by the General Assembly shall have been filed by the governor in the office of the secretary of state. The proposed law shall be submitted at the next regular or general election occurring subsequent to one hundred twenty-five days after the supplementary petition is filed in the form demanded by such supplementary petition which form shall be either as first petitioned for or with any amendment or amendments which may have been incorporated therein by either branch or by both branches, of the General Assembly. If a proposed law so submitted is approved by a majority of the electors voting thereon, it shall be the law and shall go into effect as herein provided in lieu of any amended form of said law which may have been passed by the General Assembly, and such amended law passed by the General Assembly shall not go into effect until and unless the law proposed by supplementary petition shall have been rejected by the electors. All such initiative petitions, last above described, shall have printed across the top thereof, in case of proposed laws: "Law Proposed by Initiative Petition First to be Submitted to the General Assembly." Ballots shall be so printed as to permit an affirmative or negative vote upon each measure submitted to the electors. Any proposed law or amendment to the constitution submitted to the electors as provided in section la and section 1b, if approved by a majority of the electors voting thereon, shall take effect thirty days after the election at which it was approved and shall be published by the secretary of state. If conflicting proposed laws or conflicting proposed amendments to the constitution shall be approved at the same election by a majority of the total number of votes cast for and against the same, the one receiving the highest number of affirmative votes shall be the law, or in the case of amendments to the constitution shall be the amendment to the constitution. No law proposed by initiative petition and approved by the electors shall be subject to the veto of the governor.

Section 1c. Referendum to Challenge Laws Enacted by General Assembly

The second aforestated power reserved by the people is designated the referendum, and the signatures of six per centum of the electors shall be required upon a petition to order the submission to the electors of the state for their approval or rejection, of any law, section of any law or any item in any law appropriating money passed by the General Assembly. No law passed by the General Assembly shall go into effect until ninety days after it shall have been filed by the governor in the office of the secretary of state, except as herein provided. When a petition, signed by six per centum of the electors of the state and verified as herein provided, shall have been filed with the secretary of state within ninety days after any law shall have been filed by the governor in the office of the secretary of state, ordering that such law, section of such law or any item in such law appropriating money be submitted to the electors of the state for their approval or rejection, the secretary of state shall submit to the electors of the state for their approval or rejection such law, section or item, in the manner herein provided, at the next succeeding regular or general election in any year occurring subsequent to one hundred twenty-five days after the filing of such petition, and no such law, section or item shall go into effect until and unless approved by a majority of those voting upon the same. If, however, a referendum petition is filed against any such section or item, the remainder of the law shall not thereby be prevented or delayed from going into effect.

Section 1d. Emergency Laws; Not Subject to Referendum

Laws providing for tax levies, appropriations for the current expenses of the state government and state institutions, and emergency laws necessary for the immediate preservation of the public peace, health or safety, shall go into immediate effect. Such emergency laws upon a yea and nay vote must receive the vote of two thirds of all the members elected to each branch of the General Assembly, and the reasons for such necessity shall be set forth in one section of the law, which section shall be passed only upon a yea and nay vote, upon a separate roll call thereon. The laws mentioned in this section shall not be subject to the referendum.

Section 1e. Powers; Limitation of Use

(A) The powers defined herein as the "initiative" and "referendum" shall not be used to pass a law authorizing any classification of property for the purpose of levying different rates of taxation thereon or of authorizing the levy of any single tax on land or land values or land sites at a higher rate or by a different rule than is or may be applied to improvements thereon or to personal property.

(B)(1) Restraint of trade or commerce being injurious to this state and its citizens, the power of the initiative shall not be used to pass an amendment to this constitution that would grant or create a monopoly, oligopoly, or cartel, specify or determine a tax rate, or confer a commercial interest, commercial right, or commercial license to any person, nonpublic entity, or group of persons or nonpublic entities, or any combination thereof, however organized, that is not then available to other similarly situated persons or nonpublic entities.

(2) If a constitutional amendment proposed by initiative petition is certified to appear on the ballot and, in the opinion of the Ohio ballot board, the amendment would conflict with division (B)(1) of this section, the board shall prescribe two separate questions to appear on the ballot, as follows:

(a) The first question shall be as follows:

"Shall the petitioner, in violation of division (B)(1) of Section 1e of Article II of the Ohio Constitution, be authorized to initiate a constitutional amendment that grants or creates a monopoly, oligopoly, or cartel, specifies or determines a tax rate, or confers a commercial interest, commercial right, or commercial license that is not available to other similarly situated persons?"

(b) The second question shall describe the proposed constitutional amendment.

(c) If both questions are approved or affirmed by a majority of the electors voting on them, then the constitutional amendment shall take effect. If only one question is approved or affirmed by a majority of the electors voting on it, then the constitutional amendment shall not take effect.

(3) If, at the general election held on November 3, 2015, the electors approve a proposed constitutional amendment that conflicts with division (B)(1) of this section with regard to the creation of a monopoly, oligopoly, or cartel for the sale, distribution, or other use of any federal Schedule I controlled substance, then notwithstanding any severability provision to the contrary, that entire proposed constitutional amendment shall not take effect. If, at any subsequent election, the electors approve a proposed constitutional amendment that was proposed by an initiative petition, that conflicts with division (B)(1) of this section, and that was not subject to the procedure described in division (B)(2) of this section, then notwithstanding any severability provision to the contrary, that entire proposed constitutional amendment shall not take effect.

(C) The supreme court of Ohio shall have original, exclusive jurisdiction in any action that relates to this section.

Section 1f. Power of Municipalities

The initiative and referendum powers are hereby reserved to the people of each municipality on all questions which such municipalities may now or hereafter be authorized by law to control by legislative action; such powers shall be exercised in the manner now or hereafter provided by law.

Section 1g. Petition Requirements and Preparation; Submission; Ballot Language; by Ohio Ballot Board

Any initiative, supplementary, or referendum petition may be presented in separate parts but each part shall contain a full and correct copy of the title, and text of the law, section or item thereof sought to be referred, or the proposed law or proposed amendment to the constitution. Each signer of any initiative, supplementary, or referendum petition must be an elector of the state and shall place on such petition after his name the date of signing and his place of residence. A signer residing outside of a municipality shall state the county and the rural route number, post office address, or township of his residence. A resident of a municipality shall state the street and number, if any, of his residence and the name of the municipality or the post office address. The names of all signers to such petitions shall be written in ink, each signer for himself. To each part of such petition shall be attached the statement of the circulator, as may be required by law, that he witnessed the affixing of every signature. The secretary of state shall determine the sufficiency of the signatures not later than one hundred five days before the election. The Ohio supreme court shall have original, exclusive jurisdiction over all challenges made to petitions and signatures upon such petitions under this section. Any challenge to a petition or signature on a petition shall be filed not later than ninety-five days before the day of the election. The court shall hear and rule on any challenges made to petitions and signatures not later than eighty-five days before the election. If no ruling determining the petition or signatures to be insufficient is issued at least eighty-five days before the election, the petition and signatures upon such petitions shall be presumed to be in all respects sufficient. If the petitions or signatures are determined to be insufficient, ten additional days shall be allowed for the filing of additional signatures to such petition. If additional signatures are filed, the secretary of state shall determine the sufficiency of those additional signatures not later than sixty-five days before the election. Any challenge to the additional signatures shall be filed not later than fifty-five days before the day of the election. The court shall hear and rule on any challenges made to the additional signatures not later than forty-five days before the election. If no ruling determining the additional signatures to be insufficient is issued at least forty-five days before the election, the petition and signatures shall be presumed to be in all respects sufficient. No law or amendment to the constitution submitted to the electors by initiative and supplementary petition and receiving an affirmative majority of the votes cast thereon, shall be held unconstitutional or void on account of the insufficiency of the petitions by which such submission of the same was procured; nor shall the rejection of any law submitted by referendum petition be held invalid for such insufficiency. Upon all initiative, supplementary, and referendum petitions provided for in any of the sections of this article, it shall be necessary to file from each of one-half of the counties of the state, petitions bearing the signatures of not less than one-half of the designated percentage of the electors of such county. A true copy of all laws or proposed laws or proposed amendments to the constitution, together with an argument or explanation, or both, for, and also an argument or explanation, or both, against the same, shall be prepared. The person or persons who prepare the argument or explanation, or both, against any law, section, or item, submitted to the electors by referendum petition, may be named in such petition and the persons who prepare the argument or explanation, or both, for any proposed law or proposed amendment to the constitution may be named in the petition proposing the same. The person or persons who prepare the argument or explanation, or both, for the law, section, or item, submitted to the electors by referendum petition, or against any proposed law submitted by supplementary petition, shall be named by the General Assembly, if in session, and if not in session then by the governor. The law, or proposed law, or proposed amendment to the constitution, together with the arguments and explanations, not exceeding a total of three hundred words for each, and also the arguments and explanations, not exceeding a total of three hundred words against each, shall be published once a week for three consecutive weeks preceding the election, in at least one newspaper of general circulation in each county of the state, where a newspaper is published. The secretary of state shall cause to be placed upon the ballots, the ballot language for any such law, or proposed law, or proposed amendment to the constitution, to be submitted. The ballot language shall be prescribed by the Ohio ballot board in the same manner, and subject to the same terms and conditions, as apply to issues submitted by the general assembly pursuant to Section 1 of Article XVI of this constitution: The ballot language shall be so prescribed and the secretary of state shall cause the ballots so to be printed as to permit an affirmative or negative vote upon each law, section of law, or item in a law appropriating money, or proposed law, or proposed amendment to the constitution. The style of all laws submitted by initiative and supplementary petition shall be: "Be it Enacted by the People of the State of Ohio," and of all constitutional amendments: "Be it Resolved by the People of the State of Ohio." The basis upon which the required number of petitioners in any case shall be determined shall be the total number of votes cast for the office of governor at the last preceding election therefore. The foregoing provisions of this section shall be self-executing, except as herein otherwise provided. Laws may be passed to facilitate their operation but in no way limiting or restricting either such provisions or the powers herein reserved.

Section 2. Election and Term of State Legislators

Representatives shall be elected biennially by the electors of the respective House of Representatives districts; their term of office shall commence on the first day of January next thereafter and continue two years. Senators shall be elected by the electors of the respective Senate districts; their terms of office shall commence on the first day of January next after their election. All terms of senators which commence on the first day of January, 1969 shall be four years, and all terms which commence on the first day of January, 1971 shall be four years. Thereafter, except for the filling of vacancies for unexpired terms, senators shall be elected to and hold office for terms of four years. No person shall hold the office of State Senator for a period longer than two successive terms of four years. No person shall hold the office of State Representative for a period longer than four successive terms of two years. Terms shall be considered successive unless separated by a period of four or more years. Only terms beginning on or after January 1, 1993 shall be considered in determining an individual's eligibility to hold office. In determining the eligibility of an individual to hold office in accordance with this article, (A) time spent in an office in fulfillment of a term to which another person was first elected shall not be considered provided that a period of at least four years passed between the time, if any, in which the individual previously held that office, and the time the individual is elected or appointed to fulfill the unexpired term; and (B) a person who is elected to an office in a regularly scheduled general election and resigns prior to the completion of the term for which he or she was elected, shall be considered to have served the full term in that office.

Section 3. Residence Requirements for State Legislators

Senators and representatives shall have resided in their respective districts one year next preceding their election, unless they shall have been absent on the public business of the United States, or of this state.

Section 4. Dual Office and Conflict of Interest Prohibited

No member of the General Assembly shall, during the term for which he was elected, unless during such term he resigns therefrom, hold any public office under the United States, or this state, or a political subdivision thereof; but this provision does not extend to officers of a political party, notaries public, or officers of the militia or of the United States armed forces. No member of the General Assembly shall, during the term for which he was elected, or for one year thereafter, be appointed to any public office under this state, which office was created or the compensation of which was increased, during the term for which he was elected.

Section 5. Who Shall Not Hold Office

No person hereafter convicted of an embezzlement of the public funds, shall hold any office in this state; nor shall any person, holding public money for disbursement, or otherwise, have a seat in the General Assembly, until he shall have accounted for, and paid such money into the treasury.

Section 6. Powers of Each House

Each house shall be the judge of the election, returns, and qualifications of its own members. A majority of all the members elected to each house shall be a quorum to do business; but, a less number may adjourn from day to day, and compel the attendance of absent members, in such manner, and under such penalties, as shall be prescribed by law. Each house may punish its members for disorderly conduct and, with the concurrence of two-thirds of the members elected thereto, expel a member, but not the second time for the same cause. Each house has all powers necessary to provide for its safety and the undisturbed transaction of its business, and to obtain, through committees or otherwise, information affecting legislative action under consideration or in contemplation, or with reference to any alleged breach of its privileges or misconduct of its members, and to that end to enforce the attendance and testimony of witnesses, and the production of books and papers.

Section 7. Organization of Each House of the General Assembly

The mode of organizing each house of the General Assembly shall be prescribed by law. Each house, except as otherwise provided in this constitution, shall choose its own officers. The presiding officer in the Senate shall be designated as president of the Senate and in the House of Representatives as speaker of the House of Representatives. Each house shall determine its own rules of proceeding.

Section 8. Sessions of the General Assembly

Each General Assembly shall convene in first regular session on the first Monday of January in the odd-numbered year, or on the succeeding day if the first Monday of January is a legal holiday, and in second regular session on the same date of the following year. Either the governor, or the presiding officers of the General Assembly chosen by the members thereof, acting jointly, may convene the General Assembly in special session by a proclamation which may limit the purpose of the session. If the presiding officer of the Senate is not chosen by the members thereof, the president pro tempore of the Senate may act with the speaker of the House of Representatives in the calling of a special session.

Section 9. House and Senate Journals (Yeas and Nays)

Each house shall keep a correct journal of its proceedings, which shall be published. At the desire of any two members, the yeas and nays shall be entered upon the journal; and, on the passage of every bill, in either house, the vote shall be taken by yeas and nays, and entered upon the journal.

Section 10. Rights of Members to Protest

Any member of either house shall have the right to protest against any act, or resolution thereof; and such protest, and the reasons therefore, shall without alteration, commitment, or delay, be entered upon the journal.

Section 11. Filling Vacancy in House or Senate Seat

A vacancy in the Senate or in the House of Representatives for any cause, including the failure of a member-elect to qualify for office, shall be filled by election by the members of the Senate or the members of the House of Representatives, as the case may be, who are affiliated with the same political party as the person last elected by the electors to the seat which has become vacant. A vacancy occurring before or during the first twenty months of a Senatorial term shall be filled temporarily by election as provided in this section, for only that portion of the term which will expire on the thirty-first day of December following the next general election occurring in an even-numbered year after the vacancy occurs, at which election the seat shall be filled by the electors as provided by law for the remaining, unexpired portion of the term, the member-elect so chosen to take office on the first day in January next following such election. No person shall be elected to fill a vacancy in the Senate or House of Representatives, as the case may be, unless he meets the qualifications set forth in this constitution and the laws of this state for the seat in which the vacancy occurs. An election to fill a vacancy shall be accomplished, notwithstanding the provisions of section 27, Article II of this constitution, by the adoption of a resolution, while the Senate or the House of Representatives, as the case may be, is in session, with the taking of the yeas and nays of the members of the Senate or the House of Representatives, as the case may be, affiliated with the same political party as the person last elected to the seat in which the vacancy occurs. The adoption of such resolution shall require the affirmative vote of a majority of the members elected to the Senate or the House of Representatives, as the case may be, entitled to vote thereon. Such vote shall be spread upon the journal of the Senate or the House of Representatives, as the case may be, and certified to the secretary of state by the clerk thereof. The secretary of state shall, upon receipt of such certification, issue a certificate of election to the person so elected and upon presentation of such certificate to the Senate or the House of Representatives, as the case may be, the person so elected shall take the oath of office and become a member of the Senate or the House of Representatives, as the case may be, for the term for which he was so elected.

Section 12. Privilege of Members from Arrest and of Speech

Senators and representatives, during the session of the General Assembly, and in going to, and returning from the same, shall be privileged from arrest, in all cases, except treason, felony, or breach of the peace; and for any speech, or debate, in either house, they shall not be questioned elsewhere.

Section 13. Legislative Sessions to Be Public; Exceptions

The proceedings of both houses shall be public, except in cases which, in the opinion of two-thirds of those present, require secrecy.

Section 14. Power of Adjournment

Neither house shall, without the consent of the other, adjourn for more than five days, Sundays excluded; nor to any other place than that, in which the two houses are in session.

Section 15. How Bills Shall be Passed

(A) The General Assembly shall enact no law except by bill, and no bill shall be passed without the concurrence of a majority of the members elected to each house. Bills may originate in either house, but may be altered, amended, or rejected in the other.

(B) The style of the laws of this state shall be, "be it enacted by the General Assembly of the state of Ohio."

(C) Every bill shall be considered by each house on three different days, unless two-thirds of the members elected to the house in which it is pending suspend this requirement, and every individual consideration of a bill or action sus- pending the requirement shall be re-corded in the journal of the respective house. No bill may be passed until the bill has been reproduced and distributed to members of the house in which it is pending and every amendment been made available upon a member's request.

(D) No bill shall contain more than one subject, which shall be clearly expressed in its title. No law shall be revived or amended unless the new act contains the entire act revived, or the section or sections amended, and the section or sections amended shall be repealed.

(E) Every bill which has passed both houses of the General Assembly shall be signed by the presiding officer of each house to certify that the procedural requirements for passage have been met and shall be presented forthwith to the governor for his approval.

(F) Every joint resolution which has been adopted in both houses of the General Assembly shall be signed by the presiding officer of each house to certify that the procedural requirements for adoption have been met and shall forthwith be filed with the secretary of state.

Section 16. Bills to Be Signed by Governor; Veto

If the governor approves an act, he shall sign it, it becomes law and he shall file it with the secretary of state. If he does not approve it, he shall return it with his objections in writing, to the house in which it originated, which shall enter the objections at large upon its journal, and may then reconsider the vote on its passage. If three-fifths of the members elected to the house of origin vote to repass the bill, it shall be sent, with the objections of the governor, to the other house, which may also reconsider the vote on its passage. If three fifths of the members elected to the second house vote to repass it, it becomes law notwithstanding the objections of the governor, and the presiding officer of the second house shall file it with the secretary of state. In no case shall a bill be repassed by a smaller vote than is required by the constitution on its original passage. In all cases of reconsideration the vote of each house shall be determined by yeas and nays, and the names of the members voting for and against the bill shall be entered upon the journal. If a bill is not returned by the governor within ten days, Sundays excepted, after being presented to him, it becomes law in like manner as if he had signed it, unless the General Assembly by adjournment prevents its return; in which case, it becomes law unless, within ten days after such adjournment, it is filed by him, with his objections in writing, in the office of the secretary of state. The governor shall file with the secretary of state every bill not returned by him to the house of origin that becomes law without his signature. The governor may disapprove any item or items in any bill making an appropriation of money and the item or items, so disapproved, shall be void, unless repassed in the manner prescribed by this section for the repassage of a bill.

Section 17. Repealed

Section 18. Repealed

Section 19. Repealed

Section 20. Term of Office, and Compensation of Officers in Certain Cases

The General Assembly, in cases not provided for in this constitution, shall fix the term of office and the compensation of all officers; but no change therein shall affect the salary of any officer during his existing term, unless the office be abolished.

Section 21. Contested Elections

The General Assembly shall determine, by law, before what authority, and in what manner elections shall be conducted.

Section 22. Appropriations

No money shall be drawn from the treasury, except in pursuance of a specific appropriation, made by law; and no appropriation shall be made for a longer period than two years.

Section 23. Impeachments; How Instituted and Conducted

The House of Representatives shall have the sole power of impeachment, but a majority of the members elected must concur therein. Impeachments shall be tried by the Senate; and the senators, when sitting for that purpose, shall be upon oath or affirmation to do justice according to law and evidence. No person shall be convicted without the concurrence of two-thirds of the senators.

Section 24. Officers Liable to Impeachment; Consequences

The governor, judges, and all state officers, may be impeached for any misdemeanor in office; but judgment shall not extend further than removal from office, and disqualification to hold any office under the authority of this state. The party impeached, whether convicted or not, shall be liable to indictment, trial, and judgment, according to law.

Section 25. Repealed

Section 26. Laws to Have a Uniform Operation

All laws, of a general nature, shall have a uniform operation throughout the state; nor, shall any act, except such as relates to public schools, be passed, to take effect upon the approval of any other authority than the General Assembly, except, as otherwise provided in this constitution.

Section 27. Election and Appointment of Officers; Filling Vacancies

The election and appointment of all officers, and the filling of all vacancies, not otherwise provided for by this constitution, or the constitution of the United States, shall be made in such manner as may be directed by law; but no appointing power shall be exercised by the General Assembly, except as prescribed in this constitution; and in these cases, the vote shall be taken "viva voce."

Section 28. Retroactive Laws

The General Assembly shall have no power to pass retroactive laws, or laws impairing the obligation of contracts; but may, by general laws, authorize courts to carry into effect, upon such terms as shall be just and equitable, the manifest intention of parties, and officers, by curing omissions, defects, and errors, in instruments and proceedings, arising out of their want of conformity with the laws of this state.

Section 29. No Extra Compensation; Exceptions

No extra compensation shall be made to any officer, public agent, or contractor, after the service shall have been rendered, or the contract entered into; nor shall any money be paid, on any claim, the subject matter of which shall not have been provided for by preexisting law, unless such compensation, or claim, be allowed by two-thirds of the members elected to each branch of the General Assembly.

Section 30. New Counties

No new county shall contain less than four hundred square miles of territory, nor shall any county be reduced below that amount; and all laws creating new counties, changing county lines, or removing county seats, shall, before taking effect, be submitted to the electors of the several counties to be affected thereby, at the next general election after the passage thereof, and be adopted by a majority of all the electors voting at such election, in each of said counties; but any county now or hereafter containing one hundred thousand inhabitants, may be divided, whenever a majority of the voters residing in each of the proposed divisions shall approve of the law passed for that purpose; but no town or city within the same shall be divided, nor shall either of the divisions contain less than twenty thousand inhabitants.

Section 31. Compensation of Members and Officers of the General Assembly

The members and officers of the General Assembly shall receive a fixed compensation, to be prescribed by law, and no other allowance or perquisites, either in the payment of postage or otherwise; and no change in their compensation shall take effect during their term of office.

Section 32. Divorces and Judicial Power

The General Assembly shall grant no divorce, nor exercise any judicial power not herein expressly conferred.

Section 33. Mechanics' and Contractor's Liens

Laws may be passed to secure to mechanics, artisans, laborers, subcontractors and material men, their just dues by direct lien upon the property, upon which they have bestowed labor or for which they have furnished material. No other provision of the constitution shall impair or limit this power.

Section 34. Welfare of Employees

Laws may be passed fixing and regulating the hours of labor, establishing a minimum wage, and providing for the comfort, health, safety and general welfare of all employees; and no other provision of the constitution shall impair or limit this power.

Section 34a. Minimum Wage

Except as provided in this section, every employer shall pay their employees a wage rate of not less than six dollars and eighty-five cents per hour beginning January 1, 2007. On the thirtieth day of each September, beginning in 2007, this state minimum wage rate shall be increased effective the first day of the following January by the rate of inflation for the twelve month period prior to that September according to the consumer price index or its successor index for all urban wage earners and clerical workers for all items as calculated by the federal government rounded to the nearest five cents. Employees under the age of sixteen and employees of businesses with annual gross receipts of two hundred fifty thousand dollars or less for the preceding calendar year shall be paid a wage rate of not less than that established under the federal Fair Labor Standards Act or its successor law. This gross revenue figure shall be increased each year beginning January 1, 2008 by the change in the consumer price index or its successor index in the same manner as the required annual adjustment in the minimum wage rate set forth above rounded to the nearest one thousand dollars. An employer may pay an employee less than, but not less than half, the minimum wage rate required by this section if the employer is able to demonstrate that the employee receives tips that combined with the wages paid by the employer are equal to or greater than the minimum wage rate for all hours worked. The provisions of this section shall not apply to employees of a solely family owned and operated business who are family members of an owner. The state may issue licenses to employers authorizing payment of a wage rate below that required by this section to individuals with mental or physical disabilities that may otherwise adversely affect their opportunity for employment. As used in this section: "employer," "employee," "employ," "person" and "independent contractor" have the same meanings as under the federal Fair Labor Standards Act or its successor law, except that "employer" shall also include the state and every political subdivision and "employee" shall not include an individual employed in or about the property of the employer or individual's residence on a casual basis. Only the exemptions set forth in this section shall apply to this section. An employer shall at the time of hire provide an employee the employer's name, address, telephone number, and other contact information and update such information when it changes. An employer shall maintain a record of the name, address, occupation, pay rate, hours worked for each day worked and each amount paid an employee for a period of not less than three years following the last date the employee was employed. Such information shall be provided without charge to an employee or person acting on behalf of an employee upon request. An employee, person acting on behalf of one or more employees and/or any other interested party may file a complaint with the state for a violation of any provision of this section or any law or regulation implementing its provisions. Such complaint shall be promptly investigated and resolved by the state. The employee's name shall be kept confidential unless disclosure is necessary to resolution of a complaint and the employee consents to disclosure. The state may on its own initiative investigate an employer's compliance with this section and any law or regulation implementing its provisions. The employer shall make available to the state any records related to such investigation and other information required for enforcement of this section or any law or regulation implementing its provisions. No employer shall discharge or in any other manner discriminate or retaliate against an employee for exercising any right under this section or any law or regulation implementing its provisions or against any person for providing assistance to an employee or information regarding the same. An action for equitable and monetary relief may be brought against an employer by the attorney general and/or an employee or person acting on behalf of an employee or all similarly situated employees in any court of competent jurisdiction, including the common pleas court of an employee's county of residence, for any violation of this section or any law or regulation implementing its provisions within three years of the violation or of when the violation ceased if it was of a continuing nature, or within one year after notification to the employee of final disposition by the state of a complaint for the same violation, whichever is later. There shall be no exhaustion requirement, no procedural, pleading or burden of proof requirements beyond those that apply generally to civil suits in order to maintain such action and no liability for costs or attorney's fees on an employee except upon a finding that such action was frivolous in accordance with the same standards that apply generally in civil suits. Where an employer is found by the state or a court to have violated any provision of this section, the employer shall within thirty days of the finding pay the employee back wages, damages, and the employee's costs and reasonable attorney's fees. Damages shall be calculated as an additional two times the amount of the back wages and in the case of a violation of an anti-retaliation provision an amount set by the state or court sufficient to compensate the employee and deter future violations, but not less than one hundred fifty dollars for each day that the violation continued. Payment under this paragraph shall not be stayed pending any appeal. This section shall be liberally construed in favor of its purposes. Laws may be passed to implement its provisions and create additional remedies, increase the minimum wage rate and extend the coverage of the section, but in no manner restricting any provision of the section or the power of municipalities under Article XVIII of this constitution with respect to the same. If any part of this section is held invalid, the remainder of the section shall not be affected by such holding and shall continue in full force and effect.

Section 35. Workers' Compensation

For the purpose of providing compensation to workmen and their dependents, for death, injuries or occupational disease, occasioned in the course of such workmen's employment, laws may be passed establishing a state fund to be created by compulsory contribution thereto by employers, and administered by the state, determining the terms and conditions upon which payment shall be made therefrom. Such compensation shall be in lieu of all other rights to compensation, or damages, for such death, injuries, or occupational disease, and any employer who pays the premium or compensation provided by law, passed in accordance herewith, shall not be liable to respond in damages at common law or by statute for such death, injuries or occupational disease. Laws may be passed establishing a board which may be empowered to classify all occupations, according to their degree of hazard, to fix rates of contribution to such fund according to such classification, and to collect, administer and distribute such fund, and to determine all rights of claimants thereto. Such board shall set aside as a separate fund such proportion of the contributions paid by employers as in its judgment may be necessary, not to exceed one per centum thereof in any year, and so as to equalize, insofar as possible, the burden thereof, to be expended by such board in such manner as may be provided by law for the investigation and prevention of industrial accidents and diseases. Such board shall have full power and authority to hear and determine whether or not an injury, disease or death resulted because of the failure of the employer to comply with any specific requirement for the protection of the lives, health or safety of employees, enacted by the General Assembly or in the form of an order adopted by such board, and its decision shall be final; and for the purpose of such investigations and inquiries it may appoint referees. When it is found, upon hearing, that an injury, disease or death resulted because of such failure by the employer, such amount as shall be found to be just, not greater than fifty nor less than fifteen per centum of the maximum award established by law, shall be added by the board, to the amount of the compensation that may be awarded on account of such injury, disease, or death, and paid in like manner as other awards; and, if such compensation is paid from the state fund, the premium of such employer shall be increased in such amount, covering such period of time as may be fixed, as will recoup the state fund in the amount of such additional award, notwithstanding any and all other provisions in this constitution.

Section 36. Conservation of Natural Resources

Laws may be passed to encourage forestry and agriculture, and to that end areas devoted exclusively to forestry may be exempted, in whole or in part, from taxation. Notwithstanding the provisions of section 2 of Article XII, laws may be passed to provide that land devoted exclusively to agricultural use be valued for real property tax purposes at the current value such land has for such agricultural use. Laws may also be passed to provide for the deferral or recoupment of any part of the difference in the dollar amount of real property tax levied in any year on land valued in accordance with its agricultural use and the dollar amount of real property tax which would have been levied upon such land had it been valued for such year in accordance with section 2 of Article XII. Laws may also be passed to provide for converting into forest reserves such lands or parts of lands as have been or may be forfeited to the state, and to authorize the acquiring of other lands for that purpose; also, to provide for the conservation of the natural resources of the state, including streams, lakes, submerged and swamp lands and the development and regulation of water power and the formation of drainage and conservation districts; and to provide for the regulation of methods of mining, weighing, measuring and marketing coal, oil, gas and all other minerals.

Section 37. Workday and Workweek on Public Projects

Except in cases of extraordinary emergency, not to exceed eight hours shall constitute a day's work, and not to exceed forty-eight hours a week's work, for workmen engaged on any public work carried on or aided by the state, or any political subdivision thereof, whether done by contract, or otherwise.

Section 38. Removal of Officials for Misconduct

Laws shall be passed providing for the prompt removal from office, upon complaint and hearing, of all officers, including state officers, judges and members of the General Assembly, for any misconduct involving moral turpitude or for other cause provided by law; and this method of removal shall be in addition to impeachment or other method of removal authorized by the constitution.

Section 39. Regulating Expert Testimony in Criminal Trials

Laws may be passed for the regulation of the use of expert witnesses and expert testimony in criminal trials and proceedings.

Section 40. Registering and Warranting Land Titles

Laws may be passed providing for a system of registering, transferring, insuring and guaranteeing land titles by the state or by the counties thereof, and for settling and determining adverse or other claims to and interests in, lands the titles to which are so registered, insured or guaranteed, and for the creation and collection of guaranty funds by fees to be assessed against lands, the titles to which are registered; and judicial powers with right of appeal may by law be conferred upon county recorders or other officers in matters arising under the operation of such system.

Section 41. Prison Labor

Laws may be passed providing for and regulating the occupation and employment of prisoners sentenced to the several penal institutions and reformatories in the state.

Section 42. Continuity of Government Operations in Emergencies Caused by Enemy Attack

The General Assembly shall have the power and the immediate duty to pass laws to provide for prompt and temporary succession to the powers and duties of public offices, of whatever nature and whether filled by election or appointment, the incumbents of which may become unavailable for carrying on the powers and duties of such offices and to pass such other laws as may be necessary and proper for insuring the continuity of governmental operations in periods of emergency resulting from disasters caused by enemy attack.

ARTICLE III: EXECUTIVE

Section 1. Executive Department; Key State Officers

The executive department shall consist of a governor, lieutenant governor, secretary of state, auditor of state, treasurer of state, and an attorney general, who shall be elected on the first Tuesday after the first Monday in November, by the electors of the state, and at the places of voting for members of the General Assembly.

Section 1a. Joint Vote Cast for Governor and Lieutenant

In the general election for governor and lieutenant governor, one vote shall be cast jointly for the candidates nominated by the same political party or petition. The General Assembly shall provide by law for the nomination of candidates for governor and lieutenant governor.

Section 1b. Lieutenant Governor Duties Assigned by Governor

The lieutenant governor shall perform such duties in the executive department as are assigned to him by the governor and as are prescribed by law.

Section 2. Term of Office of Key State Officers

The governor, lieutenant governor, secretary of state, treasurer of state, and attorney general shall hold their offices for four years commencing on the second Monday of January, 1959. Their terms of office shall continue until their successors are elected and qualified. The auditor of state shall hold his office for a term of two years from the second Monday of January, 1961 to the second Monday of January, 1963 and thereafter shall hold this office for a four year term. No person shall hold the office of governor for a period longer than two successive terms of four years. No person shall hold any one of the offices of lieutenant governor, secretary of state, treasurer of state, attorney general, or auditor of state for a period longer than two successive terms of four years. Terms shall be considered successive unless separated by a period of four or more years. Only terms beginning on or after January 1, 1995 shall be considered in determining an individual's eligibility to hold the office of lieutenant governor, secretary of state, treasurer of state, attorney general, or auditor of state. In determining the eligibility of an individual to hold an office in accordance with this article, (A) time spent in an office in fulfillment of a term to which another person was first elected shall not be considered provided that a period of at least four years passed between the time, if any, in which the individual previously held that office, and the time the individual is elected or appointed to fulfill the unexpired term; and (B) a person who is elected to an office in a regularly scheduled general election and resigns prior to the completion of the term for which he or she was elected, shall be considered to have served the full term in that office.

Section 3. Counting Votes for Key State Officers

The returns of every election for the officers, named in the foregoing section, shall be sealed and transmitted to the seat of government, by the returning officers, directed to the president of the Senate, who, during the first week of the next regular session, shall open and publish them, and declare the result, in the presence of a majority of the members of each house of the General Assembly. The joint candidates having the highest number of votes cast for governor and lieutenant governor and the person having the number of votes for any other office shall be declared duly elected; but if any two or more have an equal and the highest number of votes for the same office or offices, one of them or any two for whom joint votes were cast for governor and lieutenant governor, shall be chosen by joint vote of both houses.

Section 4. Repealed

Section 5. Executive Power Vested in Governor

The supreme executive power of this state shall be vested in the governor.

Section 6. Governor to See that Laws Executed; May Require Written Information

He may require information, in writing from the officers in the executive department, upon any subject relating to the duties of their respective offices; and shall see that the laws are faithfully executed.

Section 7. Governor's Annual Message to General Assembly; Recommendations for Legislation

He shall communicate at every session, by message, to the General Assembly, the condition of the state, and recommend such measures as he shall deem expedient.

Section 8. Governor May Convene Special Session of Legislature with Limited Purposes

The governor on extraordinary occasions may convene the General Assembly by proclamation and shall state in the proclamation the purpose for which such special session is called, and no other business shall be transacted at such special session except that named in the proclamation or message to the General Assembly issued by the governor during said special session, but the General Assembly may provide for the expenses of the session and other matters incidental thereto.

Section 9. When Governor May Adjourn the Legislature

In case of disagreement between the two houses, in respect to the time of adjournment, he shall have the power to adjourn the General Assembly to such time as he may think proper, but not beyond the regular meetings thereof.

Section 10. Governor is Commander-in-Chief of Militia

He shall be commander-in-chief of the military and naval forces of the state, except when they shall be called into the service of the United States.

Section 11. Governor May Grant Reprieves, Commutations and Pardons

The governor shall have power, after conviction, to grant reprieves, commutations, and pardons, for all crimes and offences, except treason and cases of impeachment, upon such conditions as the governor may think proper; subject, however, to such regulations, as to the manner of applying for commutations and pardons, as may be prescribed by law. Upon conviction for treason, the governor may suspend the execution of the sentence, and report the case to the General Assembly, at its next meeting, when the General Assembly shall either pardon, commute the sentence, direct its execution, or grant a further reprieve. The governor shall communicate to the General Assembly, at every regular session, each case of reprieve, commutation, or pardon granted, stating the name and crime of the convict, the sentence, its date, and the date of the commutation, pardon, or reprieve, with the governor's reasons therefore.

Section 12. Seal of the State, and by Whom Kept

There shall be a seal of the state, which shall be kept by the governor, and used by him officially; and shall be called "The Great Seal of the State of Ohio."

Section 13. How Grants and Commissions Issued

All grants and commissions shall be issued in the name, and by the authority, of the state of Ohio; sealed with the great seal; sighed by the governor countersigned by the secretary of state.

Section 14. Who is Ineligible for Governor

No member of Congress, or other person holding office under the authority of this state, or of the United States, shall execute the office of governor, except as herein provided.

Section 15. Succession in Case of Vacancy in Office of Governor

(A) In the case of the death, conviction on impeachment, resignation, or removal, of the governor, the lieutenant governor shall succeed to the office of governor.

(B) When the governor is unable to discharge the duties of office by reason of disability, the lieutenant governor shall serve as governor until the governors disability terminates.

(C) In the event of a vacancy in the office of governor or when the governor is unable to discharge the duties of office, the line of succession to the office of governor or to the position of serving as governor for the duration of the governor's disability shall proceed from the lieutenant governor to the president of the Senate and then to the speaker of the House of Representatives.

(D) Any person serving as governor for the duration of the governor's disability shall have the powers, duties, title and compensation of the office of governor.

(E) No person shall simultaneously serve as governor and lieutenant governor, president of the Senate or speaker of the House of Representatives, nor shall any person simultaneously receive the compensations of the office of governor and that of lieutenant governor, president of the Senate, or speaker of the House of Representatives.

Section 16. Repealed

Section 17. If a Vacancy Shall Occur While Executing the Office of Governor, Who Shall Act

When a vacancy occurs in both the office of governor and lieutenant governor because of the death, conviction on impeachment, resignation, or removal of the persons elected to those offices prior to the expiration of the first twenty months of a term, a governor and lieutenant governor shall be elected at the next general election occurring in an even-numbered year after the vacancy occurs, for the unexpired portion of the term. The officer next in line of succession to the office of governor shall serve as governor from the occurrence the vacancy until the newly elected governor has qualified. If by reason of death, resignation, or disqualification, the governor-elect shall assume the office of governor at the commencement of the gubernatorial term, the lieutenant governor-elect shall assume the office of governor for the full term. If at the commencement of such term, the governor-elect fails to assume the office by reason of disability, the lieutenant governor-elect shall serve as governor until the disability of the governor elect terminates.

Section 17a. Filling a Vacancy in the Office of Lieutenant Governor

Whenever there is a vacancy in the office of the lieutenant governor, the governor shall nominate a lieutenant governor, who shall take office upon confirmation by vote of a majority of the members elected to each house of the General Assembly.

Section 18. Governor to Fill Vacancies in Key State Offices

Should the office of auditor of state, treasurer of state, secretary of state, or attorney general become vacant, for any of the causes specified in the fifteenth section of this article, the governor shall fill the vacancy until the disability is removed, or a successor is elected and qualified. Such successor shall be elected for the unexpired term of the vacant office at the first general election in an even numbered year that occurs more than forty days after the vacancy has occurred; provided, that when the unexpired term ends within one year immediately following the date of such general election, an election to fill such unexpired term shall not be held and the appointment shall be for such unexpired term.

Section 19. Compensation of Key State Officers

The officers mentioned in this article shall, at stated times, receive for their services, a compensation to be established by law, which shall neither be increased nor diminished during the period for which they shall have been elected.

Section 20. Annual Report of Executive Officers

The officers of the executive department, and of the public state institutions shall, at least five days preceding each regular session of the General Assembly, severally report to the governor, who shall transmit such reports, with his message to the General Assembly.

Section 21. Appointments to Office; Advice and Consent of Senate

When required by law, appointments to state office shall be subject to the advice and consent of the Senate. All statutory provisions requiring advice and consent of the Senate to appointments to state office heretofore enacted by the General Assembly are hereby validated, ratified and confirmed as to all appointments made hereafter, but any such provision may be altered or repealed by law. No appointment shall be consented to without concurrence of a majority of the total number of senators provided for by this constitution, except as hereinafter provided for in the case of failure of the Senate to act. If the Senate has acted upon any appointment to which its consent is required and has refused to consent, an appointment of another person shall be made to fill the vacancy. If an appointment is submitted during a session of the General Assembly, it shall be acted upon by the Senate during such session of the General Assembly, except that if such session of the General Assembly adjourns sine die within ten days after such submission without acting upon such appointment, it may be acted upon at the next session of the General Assembly. If an appointment is made after the Senate has adjourned sine die, it shall be submitted to the Senate during the next session of the General Assembly. In acting upon an appointment a vote shall be taken by a yea and nay vote of the members of the Senate and shall be entered upon its journal. Failure of the Senate to act by a roll call vote on an appointment by the governor within the time provided for herein shall constitute consent to such appointment.

Section 22. Supreme Court to Determine Disability of Governor or Governor Elect; Succession

The Supreme Court has original, exclusive, and final, jurisdiction to determine disability of the governor or governor-elect upon presentment to it of a joint resolution by the General Assembly, declaring that the governor or governor-elect is unable to discharge the powers and duties of the office of governor by reason of disability. Such joint resolution shall be adopted by a two-thirds vote of the members elected to each house. The Supreme Court shall give notice of the resolution to the governor and after a public hearing, at which all interested parties may appear and be represented, shall determine the question of disability. The court shall make its determination within twenty-one days after presentment of such resolution. If the governor transmits to the Supreme Court a written declaration that the disability no longer exists, the Supreme Court shall, after public hearing at which all interested parties may appear and be represented, determine the question of the continuation of the disability. The court shall make its determination within twenty-one days after transmittal of such declaration. The Supreme Court has original, exclusive, and final jurisdiction to determine all questions concerning succession to the office of the governor or to its powers and duties.

ARTICLE IV: JUDICIAL

Section 1. Judicial Power Vested in Court

The judicial power of the state is vested in a supreme court, courts of appeals, courts of common pleas and divisions thereof, and such other courts inferior to the Supreme Court as may from time to time be established by law.

Section 2. Organization and Jurisdiction of Supreme Court

(A) The Supreme Court shall, until otherwise provided by law, consist of seven judges, who shall be known as the chief justice and justices. In case of the absence or disability of the chief justice, the judge having the period of longest total service upon the court shall be the acting chief justice. If any member of the court shall be unable, by reason of illness, disability or disqualification, to hear, consider and decide a cause or causes, the chief justice or the acting chief justice may direct any judge of any court of appeals to sit with the judges of the Supreme Court in the place and stead of the absent judge. A majority of the Supreme Court shall be necessary to constitute a quorum or to render a judgment.

(B)(1) The Supreme Court shall have original jurisdiction in the following:

(a) Quo warranto;

(b) Mandamus;

(c) Habeas corpus;

(d) Prohibition;

(e) Procedendo;

(f) In any cause on review as may be necessary to its complete determination;

(g) Admission to the practice of law, the discipline of persons so admitted, and all other matters relating to the practice of law.

(2) The Supreme Court shall have appellate jurisdiction as follows:

(a) In appeals from the courts of appeals as a matter of right in the following:

(i) Cases originating in the courts of appeals;

(ii) Cases in which the death penalty has been affirmed;

(iii) Cases involving questions arising under the constitution of the United States or of this state.

(b) In appeals from the courts of appeals in cases of felony on leave first obtained.

(c) In direct appeals fron the courts of common pleas or other courts of record inferior to the court of appeals as a matter of right in cases in which the death penalty has been imposed.

(d) Such revisory jurisdiction of the proceedings of administrative officers or agencies as may be conferred by law;

(e) In cases of public or great general interest, the Supreme Court may direct any court of appeals to certify its record to the Supreme Court, and may review and affirm, modify, or reverse the judgment of the court of appeals;

(f) The Supreme Court shall review and affirm, modify, or reverse the judgment in any case certified by any court of appeals pursuant to section 3(B)(4) of this article.

(3) No law shall be passed or rule made whereby any person shall be prevented from invoking the original jurisdiction of the Supreme Court.

(C) The decisions in all cases in the Supreme Court shall be reported together with the reasons therefore.

Section 3: Organization and Jurisdiction of Court of Appeals

(A) The state shall be divided by law into compact appellate districts in each of which there shall be a court of appeals consisting of three judges. Laws may be passed increasing the number of judges in any district wherein the volume of business may require such additional judge or judges. In districts having additional judges, three judges shall participate in the hearing and disposition of each case. The court shall hold sessions in each county of the district as the necessity arises. The county commissioners of each county shall provide a proper and convenient place for the court of appeals to hold court.

(B)(1) The courts of appeals shall have original jurisdiction in the following:

(a) Quo warranto;

(b) Mandamus;

(c) Habeas corpus;

(d) Prohibition;

(e) Procedendo

(f) In any cause on review as may be necessary to its complete determination.

(2) Courts of appeals shall have such jurisdiction as may be provided by law to review and affirm, modify, or reverse judgments or final orders of the courts of record inferior to the court of appeals within the district, except that courts of appeals shall not have jurisdiction to review on direct appeal a judgement that imposes a sentence of death. Courts of appeals shall have such appellate jurisdiction as may be provided by law to review and affirm, modify, or reverse final orders or actions of administrative officers or agencies.

(3) A majority of the judges hearing the cause shall be necessary to render a judgment. Judgments of the courts of appeals are final except as provided in section 2(B)(2) of the article. No judgment resulting from a trial by jury shall be reversed on the weight of the evidence except by the concurrence of all three judges hearing the cause.

(4) Whenever the judges of a court of appeals find that a judgment upon which they have agreed is in conflict with a judgment pronounced upon the same question by any other court of appeals of the state, the judges shall certify the record of the case to the Supreme Court for review and final determination.

(C) Laws may be passed providing for the reporting of cases in the courts of appeals.

Section 4. Organization and Jurisdiction of Common Pleas Court

(A) There shall be a court of common pleas and such divisions thereof as may be established by law serving each county of the state. Any judge of a court of common pleas or a division thereof may temporarily hold court in any county. In the interests of the fair, impartial, speedy, and sure administration of justice, each county shall have one or more resident judges, or two or more counties may be combined into districts having one or more judges resident in the district and serving the common pleas court of all counties in the district, as may be provided by law. Judges serving a district shall sit in each county in the district as the business of the court requires. In counties or districts having more than one judge of the court of common pleas, the judges shall select one of their number to act as presiding judge, to serve at their pleasure. If the judges are unable because of equal division of the vote to make such selection, the judge having the longest total service on the court of common pleas shall serve as presiding judge until selection is made by vote. The presiding judge shall have such duties and exercise such powers as are prescribed by rule of the Supreme Court.

(B) The courts of common pleas and divisions thereof shall have such original jurisdiction over all justiciable matters and such powers of review of proceedings of administrative officers and agencies as may be provided by law.

(C) Unless otherwise provided by law, there shall be probate division and such other divisions of the courts of common pleas as may be provided by law. Judges shall be elected specifically to such probate division and to such other divisions. The judges of the probate division shall be empowered to employ and control the clerks, employees, deputies, and referees of such probate division of the common pleas courts.

Section 5. Powers and Duties of Supreme Court; Rules

(A)(1) In addition to all other powers vested by this article in the Supreme Court, the Supreme Court shall have general superintendence over all courts in the state. Such general superintending power shall be exercised by the chief justice in accordance with rules promulgated by the Supreme Court

(2) The Supreme Court shall appoint an administrative director who shall assist the chief justice and who shall serve at the pleasure of the court. The compensation and duties of the administrative director shall be determined by the court.

(3) The chief justice or acting chief justice, as necessity arises, shall assign any judge of a court of common pleas or a division thereof temporarily to sit or hold court on any other court of common pleas or division thereof or any court of appeals or shall assign any judge of a court of appeals temporarily to sit or hold court on any other court of appeals or any court of common pleas or division thereof and upon such assignment said judge shall serve in such assigned capacity until the termination of the assignment. Rules may be adopted to provide for the temporary assignment of judges to sit and hold court in any court established by law.

(B) The Supreme Court shall prescribe rules governing practice and procedure in all courts of the state, which rules shall not abridge, enlarge, or modify any substantive right. Proposed rules shall be filed by the court, not later than the fifteenth day of January, with the clerk of each house of the General Assembly during a regular session thereof, and amendments to any such proposed rules may be so filed not later than the first day of May in that session. Such rules shall take effect on the following first day of July, unless prior to such day the General Assembly adopts a concurrent resolution of disapproval. All laws in conflict with such rules shall be of no further force or effect after such rules have taken effect. Courts may adopt additional rules concerning local practice in their respective courts which are not inconsistent with the rules promulgated by the Supreme Court. The Supreme Court may make rules to require uniform record keeping for all courts of the state, and shall make rules governing the admission to the practice of law and discipline of persons so admitted.

(C) The chief justice of the Supreme Court or any judge of that court designated by him shall pass upon the disqualification of any judge of the courts of appeals or courts of common pleas or division thereof. Rules may be adopted to provide for the hearing or disqualification matters involving judges of courts established by law.

Section 6. Election of Judges; Compensation

(A)(1) The chief justice and the justices of the Supreme Court shall be elected by the electors of the state at large, for terms of not less than six years.

(2) The judges of the courts of appeals shall be elected by the electors of their respective appellate districts, for terms of not less than six years.

(3) The judges of the courts of common pleas and the divisions thereof shall be elected by the electors of the counties, districts, or, as may be provided by law, other subdivisions, in which their respective courts are located, for terms of not less than six years, and each judge of a court of common pleas or division thereof shall reside during his term of office in the county, district, or subdivision in which his court is located.

(4) Terms of office of all judges shall begin on the days fixed by law, and laws shall be enacted to prescribe the times and mode of their election.

(B) The judges of the Supreme Court, courts of appeals, courts of common pleas, and divisions thereof, and of all courts of record established by law, shall, at stated times, receive for their services such compensation as may be provided by law, which shall not be diminished during their term of office. The compensation of all judges of the Supreme Court, except that of the chief justice, shall be the same. The compensation of all judges of the courts of appeals shall be the same. Common pleas judges and judges of divisions thereof, and judges of all courts of record established by law shall receive such compensation as may be provided by law. Judges shall receive no fees or perquisites, nor hold any other office of profit or trust, under the authority of this state, or of the United States. All votes for any judge, for any elective office, except a judicial office, under the authority of this state, given by the General Assembly, or the people shall be void.

(C) No person shall be elected or appointed to any judicial office if on or before the day when he shall assume the office and enter upon the discharge of its duties he shall have attained the age of seventy years. Any voluntarily retired judge, or any judge who is retired under this section, may be assigned with his consent, by the chief justice or acting chief justice of the Supreme Court to active duty as a judge and while so serving shall receive the established compensation for such office, computed upon a per diem basis, in addition to any retirement benefits to which he may be entitled. Laws may be passed providing retirement benefits for judges.

Section 7. Repealed

Section 8. Repealed

Section 9. Repealed

Section 10. Repealed

Section 11. Repealed

Section 12. Repealed

Section 13. Vacancy in Office of Judge, How Filled

In case the office of any judge shall become vacant, before the expiration of the regular term for which he was elected, the vacancy shall be filled by appointment by the governor, until a successor is elected and has qualified; and such successor shall be elected for the unexpired term, at the first general election for the office which is vacant that occurs more than forty days after the vacancy shall have occurred; provided, however, that when the unexpired term ends within one year immediately following the date of such general election, an election to fill such unexpired term shall not be held and the appointment shall be for such unexpired term.

Section 14. Repealed

Section 15. Changing Number of Judges; Establishing Other Courts

Laws may be passed to increase or diminish the number of judges of the Supreme Court, to increase beyond one or diminish to one the number of judges of the court of common pleas in any county, and to establish other courts, whenever two-thirds of the members elected to each house shall concur therein; but no such change, addition or diminution shall vacate the office of any judge; and any existing court heretofore created by law shall continue in existence until otherwise provided.

Section 16. Repealed

Section 17. Judges Removable

Judges may be removed from office, by concurrent resolution of both houses of the General Assembly, if two-thirds of the members, elected to each house, concur therein; but, no such removal shall be made, except upon complaint, the substance of which shall be entered on the journal, nor, until the party charged shall have had notice thereof, and an opportunity to be heard.

Section 18. Powers and Jurisdiction of Judges

The several judges of the Supreme Court, of the common pleas, and of such other courts as may be created, shall, respectively, have and exercise such power and jurisdiction, at chambers, or otherwise, as may be directed by law.

Section 19. Courts of Conciliation

The General Assembly may establish courts of conciliation, and prescribe their powers and duties; but such courts shall not render final judgment in any case, except upon submission, by the parties, of the matter in dispute, and their agreement to abide such judgment.

Section 20. Style of Process, Prosecution, and Indictment
The style of all process shall be, "The state of Ohio;" all prosecutions shall be carried on, in the name, and by the authority, of the state of Ohio; and all indictments shall conclude, "against the peace and dignity of the state of Ohio."

Section 21/22. Supreme Court Commission

A commission, which shall consist of five members, shall be appointed by the governor, with the advice and consent of the Senate, the members of which shall hold office for the term of three years from and after the first day of February, 1876, to dispose of such part of the business then on the dockets of the Supreme Court, as shall, by arrangement between said commission and said court, be transferred to such commission; and said commission shall have like jurisdiction and power in respect to such business as are or may be vested in said court; and the members of said commission shall receive a like compensation for the time being, with the judges of said court. A majority of the members of said commission shall be necessary to form a quorum or pronounce a decision, and its decision shall be certified, entered, and enforced as the judgments of the Supreme Court, and at the expiration of the term of said commission, all business undisposed of shall by it be certified to the Supreme Court and disposed of as if said commission had never existed. The clerk and reporter of said court shall be the clerk and reporter of said commission, and the commission shall have such other attendants not exceeding in number those provided by law for said court, which attendants said commission may appoint and remove at its pleasure. Any vacancy occurring in said commission, shall be filled by appointment of the governor, with the advice and consent of the Senate, if the Senate be in session, and if the Senate be not in session, by the governor, but in such last case, such appointment shall expire at the end of the next session of the General Assembly. The General

Assembly may, on application of the Supreme Court duly entered on the journal of the court and certified, provide by law, whenever two-thirds of such [each] house shall concur therein, from time to time, for the appointment, in like manner, of a like commission with like powers, jurisdiction and duties; provided, that the term of any such commission shall not exceed two years, nor shall it be created oftener than once in ten years.

Section 23. Judges in Less Populous Counties; Service on More than One Court

Laws may be passed to provide that in any county having less than forty thousand population, as determined by the next preceding federal census, the board of county commissioners of such county, by a unanimous vote or ten percent of the number of electors of such county voting for governor at the next preceding election, by petition, may submit to the electors of such county the question of providing that in such county the same person shall serve as judge of the court of common pleas, judge of the probate court, judge of the juvenile court, judge of the municipal court, and judge of the county court, or of two or more of such courts. If a majority of the electors of such county vote in favor of such proposition, one person shall thereafter be elected to serve in such capacities, but this shall not affect the right of any judge then in office from continuing in office until the end of the term for which he was elected. Elections may be had in the same manner to discontinue or change the practice of having one person serve in the capacity of judge of more than one court when once adopted.

ARTICLE V: ELECTIVE FRANCHISE

Section 1. Who May Vote

Every citizen of the United States, of the age of eighteen years, who has been a resident of the state, county, township, or ward, such time as may be provided by law, and has been registered to vote for thirty days, has the qualifications of an elector, and is entitled to vote at all elections. Any elector who fails to vote in at least one election during any period of four consecutive years shall cease to be an elector unless he again registers to vote.

Section 2. By Ballot

All elections shall be by ballot.

Section 2a. Names of Candidates on Ballot
The names of all candidates for an office at any election shall be arranged in a group under the title of that office. The General Assembly shall provide by law the means by which ballots shall give each candidate's name reasonably equal position by rotation or other comparable methods to the extent practical and appropriate to the voting procedure used. At any election in which a candidate's party designation appears on the ballot, the name or designation of each candidate's party, if any, shall be printed under or after each candidate's name in less prominent type face than that in which the candidate's name is printed. An elector may vote for candidates (other than candidates for electors of president and vice-president of the United States, and other than candidates for governor and lieutenant governor) only and in no other way than by indicating his vote for each candidate separately from the indication of his vote for any other candidate.

Section 3. Repealed

Section 4. Exclusion from Franchise

The General Assembly shall have power to exclude from the privilege of voting, or of being eligible to office, any person convicted of a felony.

Section 5. Repealed

Referred to those persons not considered residents of the state.

Section 6. Idiots or Insane Persons

No idiot, or insane person, shall be entitled to the privileges of an elector.

Section 7. Primary Elections

All nominations for elective state, district, county and municipal offices shall be made at direct primary elections or by petition as provided by law, and provision shall be made by law for a preferential vote for United States senator, but direct primaries shall not be held for the nomination of township officers or for the officers of municipalities of less than two thousand population, unless petitioned for by a majority of the electors of such township or municipality. All delegates from this state to the national conventions of political parties shall be chosen by direct vote of the electors in a manner provided by law. Each candidate for such delegate shall state his first and second choices for the presidency, but the name of no candidate for the presidency shall be so used without his written authority.

Section 8. Term Limits for U.S. Senators and Representatives

No person shall hold the office of United States Senator from Ohio for a period longer that two successive terms of six years. No person shall hold the office of United States Representative from Ohio for a period longer than four successive terms of two years. Terms shall be considered successive unless separated by a period of four or more years. Only terms beginning on or after January 1, 1993 shall be considered in determining an individual's eligibility to hold office.

Section 9. Eligibility of Officeholders

In determining the eligibility of an individual to hold an office in accordance with this article,

(A) time spent in an office in fulfillment of a term to which another person was first elected shall not be considered provided that a period of at least four years passed between the time, if any, in which the individual previously held that office, and the time the individual is elected or appointed to fulfill the unexpired term, and

(B) a person who is elected to an office in a regularly scheduled general election and resigns prior to the completion of the term for which he or she was elected, shall be considered to have served the full term in that office.

ARTICLE VI: EDUCATION

Section 1. Funds for Religious and Educational Purposes

The principal of all funds, arising from the sale, or other disposition of lands, or other property, granted or entrusted to this state for educational and religious purposes, shall be used or disposed of in such manner as the General Assembly shall prescribe by law.

Section 2. School Funds

The General Assembly shall make such provisions, by taxation, or otherwise, as, with the income arising from the school trust fund, will secure a thorough and efficient system of common schools throughout the state; but no religious or other sect, or sects, shall ever have any exclusive right to, or control of, any part of the school funds of this state.

Section 3. Public School System, Boards of Education

Provision shall be made by law for the organization, administration and control of the public school system of the state supported by public funds: provided, that each school district embraced wholly or in part within any city shall have the power by referendum vote to determine for itself the number of members and the organization of the district board of education, and provision shall be made by law for the exercise of this power by such school districts.

Section 4. State Board of Education

There shall be a state board of education which shall be selected in such manner and for such terms as shall be provided by law. There shall be a superintendent of public instruction, who shall be appointed by the state board of education. The respective powers and duties of the board and of the superintendent shall be prescribed by law.

Section 5. Loans for Higher Education

To increase opportunities to the residents of the state for higher education, it is hereby determined to be in the public interest and a proper public purpose for the state to guarantee the re payment of loans made to residents of this state to assist them in meeting the expenses of attending an institution of higher education. Laws may be passed to carry into effect such purpose including the payment, when required, of any such guarantee from moneys available for such payment after first providing the moneys necessary to meet the requirements of any bonds or other obligations heretofore or hereafter authorized by any section of the constitution. Such laws and guarantees shall not be subject to the limitations or requirements of Article VIII or of Section 11 of Article XII of the constitution. Amended Substitute House Bill No. 618 enacted by the General Assembly on July 11, 1961, and Amended Senate Bill No. 284 enacted by the General Assembly on May 23, 1963, and all appropriations of moneys made for the purpose of such enactments, are hereby validated, ratified, confirmed, and approved in all respects, and they shall be in full force and effect from and after the effective date of this section, as laws of this state until amended or repealed by law.

Section 6. Tuition Credits Program

(A) To increase opportunities to the residents of this state for higher education, it is hereby determined to be in the public interest and a proper public purpose for the state to maintain a program for the sale of tuition credits such that the proceeds of such credits purchased for the benefit of a person then a resident of this state shall be guaranteed to cover a specified amount when applied to the cost of tuition at any state institution of higher education, and the same or a different amount when applied to the cost of tuition at any other institution of higher education, as may be provided by law.

(B) The tuition credits program and the Ohio tuition trust fund previously created by law, which terms include any successor to that program or fund, shall be continued subject to the same laws, except as may hereafter be amended. To secure the guarantees required by division (A) of this section, the general assembly shall appropriate money sufficient to offset any deficiency that occurs in the Ohio tuition trust fund, at any time necessary to make payment of the full amount of any tuition payment or refund that would have been required by a tuition payment contract, except for the contract's limit of payment to money available in the trust fund. Notwithstanding section 29 of Article II of this Constitution, or the limitation of a tuition payment contract executed before the effective date of this section, such appropriations may be made by a majority of the members elected to each house of the general assembly, and the full amount of any such enhanced tuition payment or refund may be disbursed to and accepted by the beneficiary or purchaser. To these ends there is hereby pledged the full faith and credit and taxing power of the state. All assets that are maintained in the Ohio tuition trust fund shall be used solely for the purposes of that fund. However, if the program is terminated or the fund is liquidated, the remaining assets after the obligations of the fund have been satisfied in accordance with law shall be transferred to the general revenue fund of the state. Laws shall be passed, which may precede and be made contingent upon the adoption of this amendment by the electors, to provide that future conduct of the tuition credits program shall be consistent with this amendment. Nothing in this amendment shall be construed to prohibit or restrict any amendments to the laws governing the tuition credits program or the Ohio tuition trust fund that are not inconsistent with this amendment.

ARTICLE VII: PUBLIC INSTITUTIONS

Section 1. Inane, Blind, and Deaf and Dumb

Institutions for the benefit of the insane, blind, and deaf and dumb, shall always be fostered and supported by the state; and be subject to such regulations as may be prescribed by the General Assembly.

Section 2. Directors of Penitentiary, Trustees of Benevolent and Other State Institutions; How Appointed

The directors of the penitentiary shall be appointed or elected in such manner as the General Assembly may direct; and the trustees of the benevolent, and other state institutions, now elected by the General Assembly, and of such other state institutions, as may be hereafter created, shall be appointed by the governor, by and with the advice and consent of the Senate, and upon all nominations made by the governor, the question shall be taken by yeas and nays, and entered upon the journals of the Senate.

Section 3. Filling Vacancies in Directorships of State Institutions
The governor shall have power to fill all vacancies that may occur in the offices aforesaid, until the next session of the General Assembly, and, until a successor to his appointee shall be confirmed and qualified.

ARTICLE VIII: PUBLIC DEBT AND PUBLIC WORKS

Section 1. Public Debt; Limit of Deficit Spending by State

The state may contract debts to supply casual deficits or failures in revenues, or to meet expenses not otherwise provided for; but the aggregate amount of such debts, direct and contingent, whether contracted by virtue of one or more acts of the General Assembly, or at different periods of time, shall never exceed seven hundred and fifty thousand dollars; and the money, arising from the creation of such debts, shall be applied to the purpose for which it was obtained, or to repay the debts so contracted, and to no other purpose whatever.

Section 2. State May Incur Debts for Defense or to Retire Outstanding Debts

In addition to the above limited power, the state may contract debts to repel invasion, suppress insurrection, defend the state in war, or to redeem the present outstanding indebtedness of the state; but the money, arising from the contracting of such debts, shall be applied to the purpose for which it was raised, or to repay such debts, and to no other purpose whatever, and all debts, incurred to redeem the present outstanding indebtedness of the state, shall be so contracted as to be payable by the sinking fund, hereinafter provided for, as the same shall accumulate.

Section 2a. Repealed

Section 2b. Adjusted Compensation for Service in World War II; World War II Veterans' Bonuses

The board of commissioners created by section 8 of Art. VIII of the Constitution of the state of Ohio, designated therein "The Commissioners of the Sinking Fund," shall, forthwith upon the adoption of this amendment, proceed to issue and sell, from time to time, bonds of the state of Ohio in such amounts of face value as it may deem necessary to provide the funds, or such part thereof, as may be required to pay the compensation and the expenses of administering this section as herein provided for, provided, however, that the aggregate total amount of face value of bonds so issued shall not exceed three hundred million dollars. The full faith and credit of the state of Ohio is hereby pledged for the payment of such bonds. All bonds so issued shall mature in thirty semiannual installments after the respective dates thereof, and the maturities thereof shall be so fixed that the total amounts of payments on account of principal and interest to be paid on each of such semiannual installment payment dates shall be approximately equal, but no such bonds shall be issued or bear dates later than the first day of April, 1951. All bonds so issued shall bear interest at such rates as the commissioners of the sinking fund may fix, which interest shall be payable semiannually Such bonds, and the interest thereon as income, shall be exempt from all taxes levied by the state of Ohio or any taxing district thereof. The bonds may, at the option of the sinking fund commission, be issued subject to call on any interest payment date at par and accrued interest. All sales of such bonds by the commissioners of the sinking fund shall be in accordance with such regulations as it shall make and promulgate, provided, however, that such bonds shall be sold only to the highest bidder or bidders therefore after notice of such sale shall have been published once each week for three consecutive weeks on the same day of each of such weeks, the first of such notices being published at least twenty-one full days before the date of sale, in a newspaper of general circulation in each of the eight most populous counties in the state of Ohio, and provided that each of such published notices shall state the day, hour and place of the sale, the total face value of the bonds to be sold, their denominations, dates, and the dates of their maturities, information relative to the rates of interest which the bonds will bear, and the dates upon which interest will be payable. The commissioners of the sinking fund shall have the right to reject any or all bids and to re-advertise and re-offer bonds for sale. Out of the proceeds of the sale of all bonds that amount which represents accrued interest, if any, shall be paid into the treasury of the state of Ohio into a fund to be known as the World War II compensation bond retirement fund. The balance shall be paid into the treasury of the state of Ohio into a fund to be known as the World War II compensation fund. The General Assembly of the state of Ohio may appropriate and cause to be paid into the World War II compensation bond retirement fund or the World War II compensation fund, out of the funds in the treasury of the state not otherwise appropriated, such amounts as it may deem proper for use upon order of the commissioners of the sinking fund for the purposes for which such funds are created as herein provided. If the General Assembly should so appropriate any funds to the World War II compensation fund prior to the time the commissioners of the sinking fund shall have issued bonds of the aggregate total amount of face value authorized in this section, the aggregate total amount of face value of bonds so authorized to be issued shall be reduced by the amount of the funds so appropriated. During the period of fifteen years beginning January 1, 1949, the treasurer of state of the state of Ohio shall without appropriation thereof by the General Assembly, transfer into said World War II compensation bond retirement fund one million dollars each month out of funds in the state treasury derived from taxes levied by the state for the purpose of providing revenues to defray the expenses of the state, excepting the taxes levied by the state by sections 5527, 5541, and 6291 of the General Code of Ohio [RC §5735.05, 5735.25, 4303.02] as the same may be in effect on the effective date of this section. To secure such monthly transfer of funds a lien is hereby created upon all funds coming into the state treasury after January 1, 1949, derived from taxes as aforesaid, which lien shall be the first and best lien upon all such funds. It shall be the duty of the treasurer of state to set aside and use for the purpose of making such monthly transfer of funds, part of each dollar received in the state treasury in each calendar year during said period of fifteen years beginning January 1, 1949, derived from taxes as aforesaid, so that the total amount of money so set aside in each of such calendar years shall be twelve million dollars, and so that the ratio which the amount of each dollar so set aside shall bear to one dollar shall be the same as the ratio which the amount of twelve million dollars shall bear to the total amount of money received in the state treasury in such calendar years derived from taxes as aforesaid. The treasurer of state shall set aside part of each dollar before paying out, transferring, or disposing of in any other manner, such dollar or any part thereof for any other purpose whatsoever, and he shall make the transfer of one million dollars each month to the World War II compensation bond retirement fund, herein-above provided for, out of said sum of twelve million dollars so set aside in each of such calendar years. The commissioners of the sinking fund shall, on or before the first day of July in each calendar year, levy and certify to the auditor of the state of Ohio a state tax on all taxable property subject to taxation on the general tax lists of all counties in the state of Ohio for such year at such rate as it shall determine to be necessary to provide, together with other money which will be available in the World War II compensation bond retirement fund, the total amount of funds which will be required in the next following calendar year for the retirement of bonds and the payment of interest payable in such year. Such levy shall be in addition to all other taxes levied now or hereafter within the period during which bonds issued pursuant to the provisions of this section shall be outstanding, by or pursuant to law or any provision of the Constitution of the state of Ohio, and shall not be considered in applying any limitation The Constitution of the State of Ohio 29 Article VIII: Public Debt and Public Works or aggregate tax rates now or hereafter within the period during which bonds issued pursuant to the provisions of this section shall be outstanding, provided by or pursuant to law or any provision of the Constitution of the state of Ohio. The auditor of state shall certify such levies to the auditor of each county in Ohio, who shall extend the same on the tax lists of his county for the year in which such levy is made and shall place same for collection on the tax duplicates of his county to be collected the same time and in the same manner as other taxes on such duplicates. Said taxes herein authorized, when collected, shall be paid into the World War II compensation bond retirement fund in the treasury of the state. The World War II compensation bond retirement fund shall be paid out, without appropriation thereof by the General Assembly of Ohio, upon the order of the commissioners of the sinking fund for the purpose of the payment, or retirement in other manner, of said bonds and interest thereon. The World War II compensation fund shall be paid out upon order of the commissioners of the sinking fund, without appropriation by the General Assembly of Ohio, in payment of the expenses of administering this section, and as compensation as follows: every person who shall have served in active duty in the armed forces of the United States at any time between December 7, 1941 and September 2, 1945, both dates inclusive, and who, at the time of commencing such service, was and had been a resident of the state of Ohio for at least one year immediately preceding the commencement of such service, and who shall have been separated from such service under honorable conditions, or who is still in such service, or who has been retired, and who was in service for a period of at least ninety days, shall be entitled to receive compensation of ten dollars for each month during which such person was in active domestic service and fifteen dollars for each month during which such person was in active foreign service within said period of time; provided, however, that any person who was serving in active duty in the armed forces of the United States on the seventh day of December, 1941, and who did not so serve at least ninety days thereafter because of a service-connected injury or death shall be deemed to have served at least ninety days within the period of time commencing December 7, 1941 and ending September 2, 1945; and provided, further, that the maximum amount of compensation payable under this section shall not be in excess of four hundred dollars; and provided, further, that no compensation shall be paid under this section to any person who shall have received from another state a bonus or compensation of a like nature as is provided under this section. No compensation shall be paid under this section to any person for any periods of time spent under penal confinement during the period of active duty. Compensation for a fraction of a month of service shall be paid on the basis of one-thirtieth of the above monthly amounts for each day of such service. Service in the merchant marine of the United States shall not be considered for the purpose of this section. 'Domestic service" as used herein means service within the continental limits of the United States (excluding Alaska). Foreign service" as used herein means service in all other places, including sea duty. Either the surviving husband or wife, or the surviving child or children, or the surviving parents or parent, of a deceased person shall be paid the same amount of compensation that such deceased person would be entitled to receive under this section, if living; provided, however, that if such deceased person's death was service-connected and in line of duty, his survivors as hereinbefore designated, shall be paid four hundred dollars regardless of the amount of compensation which such deceased person would be entitled to receive under this section, if living; provided further, that the amount of compensation payable to such survivors of such deceased person shall be payable only to one of the three groups of survivors hereinbefore designated in the order in which said groups are herein named; and provided further, that the surviving husband or wife of more than one deceased person who would be entitled to receive compensation under this section, if living, shall be paid only that amount of compensation payable by reason of the first of the deaths of such deceased persons. No sale or assignment of any right or claim to compensation under this section shall be valid, no claims of creditors shall be enforceable against rights or claims to or payments of compensation under this section, and no fees shall be charged for services in connection with the prosecution of any right or claim to compensation or the collection of any compensation under this section. The commissioners of the sinking fund shall have complete charge of making payments of the compensation provided for in this section and shall adopt and promulgate regulations governing their procedure in connection therewith, including determinations as to who are proper beneficiaries and the amounts to which such beneficiaries are entitled, determinations as to whether an applicant has the necessary residence requirements, and such other regulations as it may deem necessary and proper; provided, however, that all applications for payment of compensation under this section shall be made to the commissioners of the sinking fund before July 1, 1950. The commissioners of the sinking fund shall select and appoint such legal counsel and employees as it may deem necessary, fix their compensation and prescribe their duties, and all such appointees shall serve at its pleasure. The people of the state of Ohio declare that their enactment of this special amendment of the Constitution of the state of Ohio is to meet the specific emergency covered thereby, and they declare it to be their intention to in no manner affect or change any of the existing provisions of the said constitution except as herein set forth. The provisions of this section shall be self executing. Upon the retirement of all the bonds that may be issued hereunder and the payment of all valid claims for compensation made within the limitations of time as prescribed herein, the commissioners of the sinking fund shall make a final report to the General Assembly of Ohio, and any balance remaining in any of the funds herein created and referred to shall be disposed of as shall be provided by law.

Section 2c. Construction of State Highway System

The state may contract debts not exceeding five hundred million dollars for the purpose of providing moneys for acquisition of rights-of-way and for construction and reconstruction of highways on the state highway system. Not more than one hundred twenty-five million dollars of the debt authorized by this section shall be contracted within any calendar year, and no part of such debt shall be contracted after the thirtyfirst day of March, 1962. The principal amount of any part of such debt at any time contracted shall be paid in substantially equal semiannual or annual installments, beginning not later than eighteen months after such debt is contracted, and in such number of installments that the entire debt shall be discharged not later than the year 1972. Securities evidencing the debt authorized by this section shall bear interest and shall be sold upon such terms as may be prescribed by law. Both the principal of such debt and the interest thereon shall be exempt from taxation by this state or by any taxing subdivision thereof. Moneys raised under the authority of this section shall be expended only to provide adequate highways, including the acquisition of rights-of-way and including participation therein with the federal government, municipal corporations, counties and other legally authorized participants, but excluding costs of planning and supervision by the state. All construction shall be done by contract as shall be provided by law. No part of such proceeds shall be appropriated except to meet the requirements of programs or schedules of acquisition of rights-of- way, highway construction and reconstruction which the governor, or other highway authority with the concurrence of the governor, shall submit to the General Assembly before such appropriations are made. Such appropriations shall be made only for major thoroughfares of the state highway system and urban extensions thereof. The debt contracted under the authority of this section shall be paid by revenue bonds issued by the state of Ohio as provided by law, secured by a pledge of moneys derived from fees, excises or license taxes, levied by the state of Ohio, relating to registration, operation, or use of vehicles on public highways, or to fuels used for propelling such vehicles, and a sufficient amount thereof shall be set aside each year, before any other distribution is made, to pay the interest on the outstanding debt and principal of such debt becoming due in that year, without other appropriations, but according to regulations to be established by law. The General Assembly shall meet on the second Monday in January, 1954, for the sole purpose of enacting laws Pursuant to this section.

Section 2d. Korean War Veterans' Bonuses

The board of commissioners created by section 8 of Article VIII of the Ohio Constitution designated therein "The Commissioners of the Sinking Fund," shall, forthwith upon the adoption of this amendment, proceed to issue and sell, from time to time, bonds of the state of Ohio in such amounts of face value as are necessary to provide the funds, or such part thereof, as may be required to pay the compensation and the expenses of administering this section as herein provided for, provided that the aggregate total amount of face value of bonds so issued shall not exceed ninety million dollars. The full faith and credit of the state of Ohio is hereby pledged for the payment of such bonds. All bonds so issued shall mature in thirty semiannual installments commencing not later than two years after the respective dates thereof. The maturities thereof shall be so fixed that the total amounts of payments on account of principal and interest to be paid on each of such semiannual installment payment dates shall be substantially equal. No such bonds shall be issued or bear dates later than the first day of April, 1959. All bonds so issued shall bear interest at such rates as the commissioners of the sinking fund may fix, which interest shall be payable semiannually Such bonds, and the interest thereon as income, shall be exempt from all taxes levied by the state of Ohio or any taxing district thereof. The bonds may, at the option of the Commissioners of the Sinking Fund, be issued subject to call on any interest payment date at par and accrued interest. All sales of such bonds by the Commissioners of the Sinking Fund shall be in accordance with such regulations as it shall make and promulgate, provided that such bonds shall be sold only to the highest bidder or bidders therefore after notice of such sale shall have been published once each week for three consecutive weeks on the same day of each of such weeks, the first of such notices being published at least twenty-one full days before the date of sale, in a newspaper of general circulation in each of the eight most populous counties in the state of Ohio, and provided that each of such published notices shall state the day, hour and place of the sale, the total face value of the bonds to be sold, their denominations, dates, and the dates of their maturities, information relative to the rates of interest which the bonds will bear, and the dates upon which interest will be payable. The Commissioners of the Sinking Fund shall have the right to reject any or all bids and to re-advertise and re-offer bonds for sale. Out of the proceeds of the sale of all bonds that amount which represents accrued interest, if any, shall be paid into the treasury of the state of Ohio into a fund to be known as The Korean Conflict Compensation Bond Retirement Fund. The balance shall be paid into the treasury of the state of Ohio into a fund to be known as The Korean Conflict Compensation Fund. The General

Assembly of the state of Ohio may appropriate and cause to be paid into The Korean Conflict Compensation Bond Retirement Fund or The Korean Conflict Compensation Fund, out of the funds in the treasury of the state not otherwise appropriated, such amount as is proper for use upon order of the Commissioners of the Sin king Fund for the purposes for which such funds are created as herein provided If the General Assembly should so appropriate any funds to The Korean Conflict Compensation Fund prior to the time the Commissioners of the Sinking Fund shall have issued bonds of the aggregate total amount of face value authorized in this section, the aggregate total amount of face value of bonds so authorized to be issued shall be reduced by the amount of the funds so appropriated. The Commissioners of the Sinking Fund shall, on or before the first day of July in each calendar year, levy and certify to the auditor of the state of Ohio a state tax on all taxable property subject to taxation on the general tax lists of all counties in the state of Ohio for such year at such rate as it shall determine to be necessary to provide, together with other money which will be available in The Korean Conflict Compensation Bond Retirement Fund, the total amount of funds which will be required in the next following calendar year for the retirement of bonds and the payment of interest payable in such year. Such levy shall be in addition to all other taxes levied now or hereafter within the period during which bonds issued pursuant to the provisions of this section shall be outstanding, by or pursuant to law or any provision of the Ohio Constitution shall not be considered in applying any limitation or aggregate tax rates now or hereafter the period during which bonds issued pursuant to the provisions of this section shall be outstanding, provided by or pursuant to law or any provision of the Ohio Constitution. The auditor of state shall certify such levies to the auditor of each county in the state of Ohio, who shall extend the same on the tax lists of his county for the year in which such levy is made and shall place the same for collection on the tax duplicates of his county to be collected at the same time and in the same manner as other taxes on such duplicates. Said taxes herein authorized, when collected, shall be paid into The Korean Conflict Compensation

Bond Retirement Fund in the treasury of the state. The Korean Conflict Compensation Bond Retirement Fund shall be paid out, without appropriation thereof by the General Assembly of Ohio upon the order of the Commissioners of the Sinking Fund for the purpose of the payment, or retirement in other manner, of said bonds and interest thereon. The Korean Conflict Compensation Fund shall be paid out upon order of the Commissioners of the Sinking Fund, without appropriation by the General Assembly of Ohio, in payment of the expenses of administering this section, and as compensation as follows: Every person who shall have served on active duty in the armed forces of the United States at any time between June 25th 1950, and July 19, 1953, both dates inclusive, and who at the time of commencing such service, was and had been a resident of the state of Ohio for at least one year immediately preceding the commencement of such service, and

(1) who shall have been separated from such service under honorable conditions or

(2) who is still in such service, or

(3) who has been retired, shall be entitled to receive compensation of ten dollars for each month during which such person was in active domestic service and of fifteen dollars for each month during which such person was in active foreign service within said period of time; provided that the maximum amount of compensation payable under this section shall not be in excess of four hundred dollars; and provided that no compensation shall be paid under this section to any person who shall have received from another state a bonus or compensation of a like nature as is provided under this section. Compensation for a fraction of a month of service shall be paid on the basis of one-thirtieth of the above monthly amounts for each day of such service. Service in the Merchant Marine of the United States shall not be considered for the purpose of this section. "Domestic service" as used herein, means service within the continental limits of the United States excluding Alaska and sea duty. "Foreign service" as used herein means service in all other places, including sea duty. No compensation shall be paid under this section to any person for any periods of time spent under penal confinement during the period of active duty. Either the surviving husband or wife, or the surviving child or children, or the surviving parents or parent, including persons standing in loco parentis for one year preceding commencement of service in the armed forces of the United States, of a deceased person shall be paid the same amount of compensation that such deceased person would have been entitled to receive under this section, if living; provided that if such deceased person's death is determined to have been service-connected by the Veteran's Administration of the United States government, his survivors as herein designated, shall be entitled to four hundred dollars regardless of the amount of compensation which such deceased person would have been entitled to receive under this section if living; provided that the amount of compensation payable to such survivors of such deceased person shall be payable only to one of the three groups of survivors herein designated in the order in which said groups are named. No sale or assignment of any right or claim to compensation under this section shall be valid, no claims of creditors shall be enforceable against rights or claims to or payments of compensation under this section, and no fees shall be charged for services in connection with the prosecution of any right or claim to compensation or the collection of any compensation under this section. The Commissioners of the Sinking Fund shall have complete charge of making payments of the compensation provided for in this section and shall adopt and promulgate regulations governing their procedure in connection therewith, including determinations as to who are proper beneficiaries and the amounts to which such beneficiaries are entitled, determinations as to whether an applicant has the necessary residence requirements, and such other regulations that are necessary and proper; provided that all applications for payment of compensation under this section shall be made to the Commissioners of the Sinking Fund before January 1, 1959. The Commissioners of the Sinking Fund shall select and appoint such legal counsel and employees that are necessary, fix their compensation and prescribe their duties, and all such appointees shall serve at its pleasure. The Commissioners of the Sinking Fund shall permit review of individual records of claims by representatives of recognized veterans organizations when authorized to do so by the applicant. There is hereby transferred, out of the fund known as the "World War II Compensation Fund", created by section 2b of Article VIII of the Ohio Constitution, the sum of four million dollars, to The Korean Conflict Compensation Fund, for the purpose of defraying the immediate cost of administration and compensation. The people of the state of Ohio declare that their enactment of this special amendment of the Ohio Constitution is to meet the specific emergency covered thereby, and they declare it to be their intention to in no manner affect or change any of the existing provisions of the said constitution except as herein set forth. The provisions of this section shall be self executing. Upon payment of all valid claims for compensation made within the limitations of time as prescribed herein, the Commissioners of the Sinking Fund may transfer any funds in The Korean Conflict Compensation Fund to The Korean Conflict Compensation Bond Retirement Fund. Upon retirement of all of the bonds that may be issued hereunder and the payment of all valid claims for compensation made within the limitations of time as prescribed herein, the Commissioners of the Sinking Fund shall make a final report to the General Assembly of Ohio, and any balance remaining in any of the funds herein created and referred to shall be disposed of as shall be provided by law.

Section 2e. Providing Means for Securing Funds for Highway and Public Building Construction

The state may borrow money and issue bonds or other obligations therefore for the purpose of acquiring, constructing, reconstructing and otherwise improving and equipping buildings and structures, excluding highways, and for the purpose of acquiring sites for such buildings and structures, for the penal, correctional, mental, and welfare institutions of the state; for the state supposed universities and colleges of the state; for class room facilities to be leased or sold by the state to public school districts unable within limitations provided by law to provide adequate facilities without assistance from the state, and for state offices; provided that the aggregate total amount of such borrowing under authority of this section shall not exceed $150,000,000. Not more than thirty million dollars of such borrowing shall be contracted within any calendar year. Note more than thirty million dollars of such borrowing shall be contracted within any calendar year. No part of such borrowing shall be contracted after the last day of December 1964. All bonds or other obligations issued pursuant to this section shall mature within twenty years from date of issue. Not more than $75,000,000 of the total expenditure from such borrowing shall be for acquisition, construction, reconstruction and other improvement and equipping of buildings and structures, or for acquisition of sites for such buildings and structures, for the state supported universities and colleges, public school class room facilities and state offices; and not more than $75,000,000 of the total expenditure from such borrowing shall be for acquisition, construction, reconstruction and other improvement and equipping of buildings and structures, or for acquisition of sites for such buildings and structures, for the penal, correctional, mental, and welfare institutions of the state. The faith and credit of the state are hereby pledged for the payment of such bonds or other obligations and the interest thereon, and they shall be payable from all excises and taxes of the state, except ad valorem taxes on real and personal property, income taxes, and fees, excises, or license taxes relating to registration, operation, or use of vehicles on public highways, or to fuels used for propelling such vehicles. During the period beginning with the effective date of the first authorization to issue bonds or other obligations under authority of this section and ending on the last day of December 1964, and continuing during such time as such bonds or other obligations are outstanding, and moneys in the capital improvements bond retirement fund are insufficient to pay all interest, principal and charges for the issuance and retirement of such bonds and other obligations, there shall be levied, for the purpose of paying interest, principal, and charges for the issuance and retirement of such bonds and other obligations, an excise tax on sales of cigarettes at the rate of one-half cent on each ten cigarettes or fractional part thereof, and an excise tax on the use, consumption, or storage for consumption of cigarettes by consumers in this state at the rate of one-half cent on each ten cigarettes or fractional part thereof. Such tax on the use, consumption or storage for consumption of cigarettes by consumers in this state shall not be levied upon cigarettes upon which the tax on sales has been paid. The moneys received into the state treasury from the one-half cent excise tax on sales of cigarettes and from the one-half cent excise tax on the use, consumption or storage for consumption of cigarettes by consumers in this state shall be paid into the capital improvements bond retirement fund. The General Assembly of Ohio shall enact laws providing for the collection of such taxes. There is hereby created in the state treasury a fund to be known as the capital improvements bond retirement fund. The capital improvements bond retirement fund shall consist of all moneys received by the state from taxes on cigarettes levied under authority of this section, and all other moneys credited to the fund pursuant to law. Such moneys shall be expended, as provided by law, for the purpose of paying interest, principal, and charges for the issuance and retirement of bonds and other obligations issued under authority of this section. Sufficient amounts of such moneys in the capital improvements bond retirement fund are hereby appropriated for the purpose of paying interest, principal, and charges for the issuance and retirement of bonds or other obligations issued under authority of this section, without other appropriations but according to law. Any balance remaining in the capital improvements bond retirement fund after payment of all interest, principal, and charges for the issuance and retirement of bonds and other obligations issued under authority of this section, shall be disposed of as shall be provided by law. As long as any of such bonds or other obligations are outstanding there shall be levied and collected, in amounts sufficient to pay the principal of and the interest on such bonds or other obligations, excises and taxes, excluding those above excepted. The General Assembly shall meet on the third Monday of January, 1956 for the purpose of enacting laws pursuant to this section.

Section 2f. Authorizing Bond Issue to Provide School Classrooms, Support for Universities, for Recreation and Conservation and for State Buildings

In addition to the authorization in Article VIII, Section 2e, the state may borrow not to exceed two hundred fifty million dollars and issue bonds or other obligations therefore, for the purpose of acquiring, constructing, reconstructing, and otherwise improving and equipping buildings and structures, excluding highways; and for the purpose of acquiring lands and interests in lands for sites for such buildings and structures; and for the purpose of assisting in the development of the state, to acquire lands and interests in lands and to develop such lands and interests or other state lands for water impoundment sites, park and recreational uses, and conservation of natural resources; and for use in conjunction with federal grants or loans for any of such purposes. Of said amount, for the purpose of acquiring, constructing, reconstructing, and otherwise improving and equipping buildings and structures, excluding highways, and for the purpose of acquiring lands and interests in lands for sites for such buildings and structures, one hundred seventy-five million dollars shall be issued for the state supported or assisted college or universities including community colleges, municipal universities, and university branches, thirty- five million dollars shall be issued for providing classroom facilities for the public schools to be leased or sold by the state to public school districts unable, within the limitations provided by law, to provide adequate facilities without assistance from the state, and fifteen million dollars shall be issued for state functions, activities, offices, institutions, including penal, correctional, mental, and welfare, and research and development; and for the purpose of assisting in the development of the state by acquiring lands and interests in lands and to develop such lands and interests or other state lands for water impoundment sites, park and recreational uses, and conservation of natural resources twenty-five million dollars shall be issued. Not more than one hundred million dollars of such borrowing shall be contracted within any calendar year. No part of such borrowing shall be contracted after the thirty-first day of December, 1972. All bonds or other obligations issued pursuant to this section shall mature at such time or times not exceeding thirty years from date of issue and in such amounts as shall be fixed by the commissioners of the sinking fund, and shall bear interest and be sold as shall be authorized by law. Both the principal of such debt and the interest thereon shall be exempt from taxation within this state. The faith and credit of the state are hereby pledged for the payment of such bonds or other obligations, and the interest thereon. They shall be payable from all excises and taxes of the state except ad valorem taxes on real and personal property, income taxes, and fees, excises or license taxes relating to registration, operation, or use of vehicles on public highways or to fuels used for propelling such vehicles. The excises and taxes of the state from which such bonds and other obligations shall be paid shall include an excise tax on sales of cigarettes at the rate of one-half cent on each ten cigarettes or fractional part thereof, and an excise tax on the use, consumption, or storage for consumption of cigarettes by consumers in this state, at the rate of one-half cent on each ten cigarettes or fractional part thereof, which shall be levied during the period beginning with January 1, 1965, and continuing until December 31, 1972, and thereafter as long as any of such bonds and other obligations are outstanding and moneys in the separate and distinct bond retirement fund hereinafter created are insufficient to pay all interest, principal, and charges for the issuance and retirement of such bonds and other obligations. Such tax on the use, consumption, or storage for consumption of cigarettes by consumers in this state shall not be levied upon cigarettes upon which the tax on sales has been paid. The General Assembly of the state of Ohio shall enact laws providing for the collection of such taxes. The moneys received into the state treasury from such one-half cent excise tax on sales of cigarettes and from such one half cent excise tax on the use, consumption, or storage for consumption of cigarettes by consumers in this state shall be paid into a separate and distinct bond retirement fund hereby created. There shall be transferred in each year from said bond retirement fund to the capital improvements bond retirement fund created by Article VIII, Section 2e of the Constitution of the State of Ohio, from the proceeds of the levy of such excise taxes on cigarettes, such amounts as may be necessary for the payment in such year of the interest, principal, and charges of the bonds or other obligations issued pursuant to said Article VIII, Section 2e falling due in such year, to the extent that moneys in said capital improvements bond retirement fund in such year are insufficient to pay such interest, principal, and charges. The excise taxes on the sale, use, consumption or storage of cigarettes authorized to be levied by Article VIII, Section 2e of the Constitution of the State of Ohio for the payment of bonds and other obligations issued under authority of that section shall not be levied during any period that they are not required to be levied by Article VIII, Section 2e of the Constitution of the State of Ohio. Sufficient amounts of such moneys remaining in said separate and distinct bond retirement fund created by this section, after such transfers, are hereby appropriated for the purpose of paying interest, principal, and charges for the issuance and retirement of bonds and other obligations issued under authority of this section, without other appropriations but according to law. In the event the moneys in the separate and distinct bond retirement fund created by this section are at any time insufficient to pay the current interest, principal, and charges for the issuance and retirement of bonds and other obligations issued under authority of this section, then such moneys as may be required to pay such current interest, principal, and charges are hereby appropriated for those purposes, without other appropriations but according to law, from the proceeds of all excises and taxes excluding those above excepted. Provision may be made by law for the transfer and the use of any amount in said separate and distinct bond retirement fund in excess of that required in any year for payment of interest, principal, and charges for the issuance and retirement of bonds and other obligations issued under authority of said Article VIII, Section 2e and this section. Any balance remaining in the separate and distinct bond retirement fund created by this section after payment of all interest, principal, and charges for the issuance and retirement of bonds or other obligations issued under authority of this section shall be disposed of for the purposes enumerated in this section as may be provided by law. As long as any of such bonds or other obligations are outstanding there shall be levied and collected in amounts sufficient to pay the principal of and interest on such bonds or other obligations, excises and taxes, excluding those above excepted.

Section 2g. Authorizing Bond Issue or Other Obligations for Highway Construction

The state may contract debts not exceeding five hundred million dollars for the purpose of providing moneys for acquisition of rights-of-way and for construction and reconstruction of highways on the state highway system and urban extensions thereof. The principal amount of any part of such debt at any time contracted shall be paid at such time or times and in such amounts as shall be fixed by the Commissioners of the Sinking Fund provided that the entire debt shall be discharged not later than the year 1989. The bonds or other obligations evidencing the debt authorized by this section shall bear interest and shall be sold upon such terms as may be prescribed by law. Both the principal of such debt and the interest thereon shall be exempt from taxation within this state. Moneys raised under the authority of this section shall be expended only to provide adequate highways, including engineering and the acquisition of rights-of-way and including participation therein with the federal government, municipal corporations, counties and other legally authorized participants. All construction shall be done by contract as shall be provided by law. No part of such proceeds shall be appropriated except to meet the requirements of programs or schedules or acquisition of rights-of-way, highway construction and reconstruction which the governor, or other highway authority designated by law, with the concurrence of the governor, shall submit to the General Assembly before such appropriations are made. Such appropriations shall be made only for major thoroughfares of the state highway system and urban extensions thereof. The debt contracted under the authority of this section shall be evidenced by bonds or other obligations issued by the state of Ohio as provided by law. The faith and credit of the state are hereby pledged for the payment thereof and the interest thereon. Such bonds or other obligations shall be paid from moneys derived from fees, excises, or license taxes, levied by the state of Ohio, relating to registration, operation, or use of vehicles on public highways, or to fuels used for propelling such vehicles, and a sufficient amount thereof, after provision for the amounts required by Article VIII, Section 2c of the Constitution of the State of Ohio for obligations issued pursuant to that section, is hereby appropriated in each year for the purpose of paying the interest on the outstanding debt and the principal of such debt contracted under authority of this section becoming due in that year, without other appropriations, but according to regulations to be established by law. Provision may be made by law for the transfer and the use of any amount of such moneys in excess of that required, in any year, for the payment of interest on and the principal of such debt contracted under authority of this section and said section 2c.

Section 2h. Bond Issue for State Development

The state may, from time to time, borrow not to exceed two hundred ninety million dollars and issue bonds or other obligations thereof for any one or more of the following purposes: acquiring, constructing, reconstructing or otherwise improving and equipping buildings and structures of the state and state supported and assisted institutions of higher education, including those for research and development; acquiring lands and interests in lands for sites for such buildings and structures; assisting in the development of the state, to acquire and develop lands and interests in lands and develop other state lands for water impoundment sites, flood control, parks and recreational uses, or conservation of natural resources; to develop state parks and recreational facilities including the construction, reconstruction and improvement of roads and highways therein; to assist the political subdivisions of the state to finance the cost of constructing and extending water and sewerage lines and mains, for use in conjunction with federal grants or loans for any of such purposes; and for use in conjunction with other governmental entities in acquiring, constructing, reconstructing, improving, and equipping water pipelines, stream flow improvements, airports, historical or educational facilities. The aggregate total amount of such borrowing outstanding under authority of this section shall not, at any time, exceed such sum as will require, during any calendar year, more than $20,000,000 to meet the principal and interest requirements of any such bonds and other obligations, and the charges for the issuance and retirement of such bonds and other obligations, falling due that year. No part of such borrowing shall be contracted after the last day of December, 1970. All bonds or other obligations issued pursuant to this section shall mature within thirty years from the date of issue. The faith and credit of the state are hereby pledged for the payment of such bonds or other obligations or the interest thereon, and they shall be payable from all excises and taxes of the state, except ad valorem taxes on real and personal property, income taxes, and fees, excises or license taxes relating to the registration, operation, or use of vehicles on the public highways, or to fuels used for propelling such vehicles, after making provision for payment of amounts pledged from such excises and taxes for payment of bonds issued under authority of Sections 2e and 2f of this Article. During the period beginning with the effective date of the first authorization to issue bonds or other obligations under authority of this section and continuing during such time as such bonds or other obligations are outstanding and so long as moneys in the Development Bond Retirement Fund are insufficient to pay all interest, principal and charges of such bonds or other obligations issued under authority of this section and becoming due in each year, a sufficient amount of moneys derived from such excises and taxes of the state is hereby appropriated in each year for the purpose of paying the interest, principal and charges for the issuance and retirement of bonds or other obligations issued under authority of this section becoming due in that year without other appropriation but according to law. The moneys derived from such excises and taxes and hereby appropriated shall be paid into a distinct bond retirement fund designated Development Bond Retirement Fund," hereby created. Such moneys shall be expended as provided by law for the purpose of paying interest, principal and charges for the issuance and retirement of bonds and other obligations issued under authority of this section. Sufficient amounts of such moneys in the Development Bond Retirement Fund are hereby appropriated for the purpose of paying interest, principal and charges for the issuance and retirement of bonds or other obligations issued under authority of this section, so long as any of them are outstanding, without other appropriations but according to law. Any balance remaining in the Development Bond Retirement Fund after payment of all interest, principal and charges for the issuance and retirement of bonds and other obligations issued under authority of this section, shall be disposed of as shall be provided by law. As long as any of such bonds or other obligations are outstanding there shall be levied and collected, in amounts sufficient to pay the principal of and the interest on such bonds or other obligations, excises and taxes, excluding those above excepted.

Section 2i. Capital Improvement Bonds

In addition to the authorization otherwise contained in Article VIII of the Ohio Constitution, the General Assembly, in accordance with but subject to the limitations of this section, may authorize the issuance of obligations, including bonds and notes, of the state or of state institutions, boards, commissions, authorities, or other state agencies or instrumentalities for any one or more of the following public capital improvements: the construction, reconstruction, or other improvement of highways, including those on the state highway system and urban extensions thereof, those within or leading to public parks or recreational areas, and those within or leading to municipal corporations, the acquisition, construction, reconstruction, or other improvement of, and provision of equipment for, buildings, structures, or other improvements, and necessary planning and engineering, for water pollution control and abatement, including those for sewage collection, treatment, or disposal, water management, including those for water distribution, collection, supply, storage, or impoundment, and stream flow control, and flood control, state supported or assisted institutions of higher education, technical education, vocational education, juvenile correction, training and rehabilitation, parks and recreation, research and development with respect to transportation, highways, and highway transportation, mental hygiene and retardation, police and fire training, airports, and other state buildings and structures, and the acquisition and improvement of real estate and interests therein required with respect to the foregoing, including participation in any such capital improvements with the federal government, municipal corporations, counties, or other governmental entities or any one or more of them which participation may be by grants, loans or contributions to them for any of such capital improvements. It is hereby determined that such capital improvements will directly or indirectly create jobs, enhance employment opportunities, and improve the economic welfare of the people of the state. The issuance under authority of this section of obligations the holders or owners of which are given the right to have excises and taxes levied by the General Assembly for the payment of the principal thereof or interest thereon, herein called tax supported obligations, shall be subject to the following limitations. Not more than one hundred million dollars principal amount may be issued in any calendar year and not more than five hundred million dollars principal amount may be outstanding any one time for such capital improvements for highways and research and development with respect to highways and highway transportation, herein called highway obligations, provided that fifty per cent of the proceeds of the first five hundred million dollars of such tax supported highway obligations shall be used for urban extensions of state highways and highways within or leading to municipal corporations. Not more than two hundred fifty nine million dollars aggregate principal amount of such tax supported obligations may be issued for the other capital improvements aforesaid, provided that from the proceeds thereof one hundred twenty million dollars shall be used for water pollution control and abatement and water management, one hundred million dollars shall be used for higher education, technical and vocational education, and juvenile correction, training and rehabilitation, twenty million dollars shall be used for parks and recreation, and nineteen million dollars for airports, and for construction, rehabilitation and equipping of other state buildings and structures, including those for police and fire training. If tax supported obligations are issued under authority of this section to retire tax supposed obligations previously issued under authority of this section, such new obligations shall not be counted against such limits to the extent that the principal amount thereof does not exceed the principal amount of the obligations to be retired thereby. Each issue of tax supported obligations issued pursuant to this section shall mature in not more than thirty years from the date of issuance thereof, or, if issued to retire obligations issued hereunder, within thirty years from the date such debt was originally contracted. If such tax supposed obligations are issued as notes in anticipation of the issuance of bonds, provision shall be made by law for setting aside, so long as such notes are outstanding, into a special fund or funds such amounts from the sources authorized for payment of such bonds under this section as would be sufficient for payment of that amount of principal on such bonds that would have been payable during such period if such bonds, maturing during a period of thirty years, had been issued without prior issuance of such notes. Such fund or funds may be used solely for the payment of principal of such notes or of bonds in anticipation of which such notes have been issued. The faith and credit and excises of taxes of the state, excluding ad valorem taxes on real or personal property and income taxes, shall be pledged to the payment of the principal of and the interest on such tax supported obligations, sinking or bond retirement fund provisions shall be made therefore, and this section shall otherwise be implemented, all in the manner and to the extent provided by law by the General Assembly, including provisions for appropriation of pledged excises and taxes, and covenants to continue their levy, collection and application, to continue so long as such tax supported obligations are outstanding, without necessity for further appropriation notwithstanding Section 22 of Article II, Ohio Constitution; provided that the moneys referred to in Section 5a of Article XII, Ohio Constitution herein called highway user receipts, shall, after provision for payment of amounts pledged to obligations heretofore or hereafter issued under Sections 2c and 2g of this Article, be pledged to the payment of the principal of and interest on highway obligations authorized by this section but not to other obligations authorized hereby. If excises and taxes other than highway user receipts are pledged to the payment of the principal of or interest on highway obligations authorized by this section, in each year that such highway user receipts are available for such purpose, the same shall be appropriated thereto and the required application of such other excises and taxes shall be reduced in corresponding amount. The General Assembly also may authorize the issuance of revenue obligations and other obligations, the owners or holders of which are not given the right to have excises or taxes levied by the General Assembly for the payment of principal thereof or interest thereon, for such capital improvements for mental hygiene and retardation, parks and recreation, state supported and state assisted institutions of higher education, including those for technical education, water pollution control and abatement, water management, and housing of branches and agencies of state government, which obligations shall not be subject to other provisions of this section and shall not be deemed to be debts or bonded indebtedness of the state under other provisions of this constitution. Such obligations may be secured by a pledge under law, without necessity for further appropriation, of all or such portion as the General Assembly authorizes of charges for the treatment or care of mental hygiene and retardation patients, receipts with respect to parks and recreational facilities, receipts of or on behalf of state supported and state assisted institutions of higher education, or other revenues or receipts, specified by law for such purpose, of the state or its officers, departments, divisions, institutions, boards, commissions, authorities, or other state agencies instrumentalities, and this provision may be implemented by law to better provide therefore; provided, however, that any charges for the treatment or care of mental hygiene or retardation patients may be so pledged only to obligations issued for capital improvements for mental hygiene and retardation, any receipts with respect to parks and recreation may be so pledged only to obligations issued for capital improvements for parks and recreation, any receipts of or on behalf of state supported or state assisted institutions of higher education may be pledged only to obligations issued for capital improvements for state supported or state assisted institutions of higher education, and any other revenues or receipts may be so pledged only to obligations issued for capital improvements which are in whole or in part useful to, constructed by, or financed by the department, board, commission, authority, or other agency or instrumentality that receives the revenues or receipts so pledged. The authority provided by this paragraph is in addition to, cumulative with, and not a limitation upon, the authority of the General Assembly under other provisions of this constitution; such paragraph does not impair any law heretofore enacted by the General Assembly, and any obligations issued under any such law consistent with the provisions of this paragraph shall be deemed to be issued under authority of this paragraph. Both the principal of all obligations authorized under authority of this section and the interest thereon shall be exempt from taxation within this state.

Section 2j. Vietnam Conflict Compensation Fund

The board of commissioners created by section 8 of Article VIII of the Ohio Constitution shall, forthwith upon the adoption of this amendment, proceed to issue and sell, from time to time, bonds or notes of the state in such amounts of face value as are necessary to provide the funds, or such part thereof, as may be required to pay the compensation and the expenses of administering this section. The aggregate face value of bonds or notes so issued shall not exceed three hundred million dollars. The full faith and credit of the state is hereby pledged for the payment of such bonds or notes. All bonds or notes so issued shall mature in not more than fifteen years commencing not later than two years after the respective dates thereof. The bonds or notes shall mature according to schedules set forth by the commissioners but shall not mature more than fifteen years after the date of issue. No bonds or notes shall be issued or bear dates later than the first day of April, 1977. All bonds or notes shall bear interest at such rates as the commissioners determine and shall be payable semiannually. Such bonds or notes, and the interest thereon are exempt from all taxes levied by the state or any taxing district thereof. At the option of the commissioners, the bonds or notes may be issued subject to call on any interest payment date at par and accrued interest. All sales of such bonds or notes by the commissioners shall be in accordance with such regulations as the commission adopts and promulgates. Such bonds or notes shall be sold only to the highest bidder or bidders after notice of sale has been published once each week for three consecutive weeks on the same day of each week, the first of such notices being published at least twenty-one full days before the date of sale, in a newspaper of general circulation in each of the eight most populous counties in the state. Notices shall state the day, hour and place of the sale, the total face value of the bonds or notes to be sold, their denominations, dates, and the dates of their maturities, information relative to the rates of interest that the bonds or notes will bear, and the dates upon which interest will be payable. The commissioners may reject any or all bids and re-advertise and re-offer bonds or notes for sale. Out of the proceeds of the sale of all bonds or notes, that amount that represents accrued interest, if any, shall be paid into the state treasury into a fund to be known as the Vietnam Conflict Compensation Bond Retirement Fund, and the balance shall be paid into the state treasury into a fund to be known as the Vietnam Conflict Compensation Fund. The General Assembly may appropriate and cause to be paid into the Vietnam Conflict Compensation Bond Retirement Fund or the Vietnam Conflict Compensation Fund, out of the funds in the treasury not otherwise appropriated, such amount as is proper for use, upon order of the commissioners for the purposes for which such funds are created. If the General Assembly appropriates any funds to the Vietnam Conflict Compensation Fund prior to the time the commissioners have issued bonds or notes of the aggregate amount of face value authorized in this section, the aggregate amount of face value of bonds or notes so authorized to be issued shall be reduced by the amount of the funds so appropriated. On or before the first day of July in each calendar year, the commissioners shall certify to the auditor of state the total amount of funds it determines is necessary to provide, together with all other money that will be available in the Vietnam Conflict Compensation Bond Retirement Fund, for the retirement of bonds or notes and the payment of interest in the ensuing calendar year. The auditor of state shall transfer from the state general revenue fund to the Vietnam Conflict Compensation Bond Retirement Fund, without appropriation, an amount equal to the amount so certified. The Vietnam Conflict Compensation Bond Retirement Fund shall be paid out without appropriation by the General Assembly, upon the order of the commissioners for the purpose of the payment, or retirement in other manner, of said bonds or notes and interest thereon. The Vietnam Conflict Compensation Fund shall be paid out upon order of the commissioners, without appropriation by the General Assembly, in payment of the expenses of administering this section, and as compensation as follows: every person, except persons ordered to active duty for training only, who has served on active duty in the armed forces of the United States at any time between August 5, 1964 and July 1, 1973, or who has served on active duty in the armed forces of the United States in Vietnam service, and who, at the time of commencing such service, was and had been a resident of the state for at least one year immediately preceding the commencement of such service, and

(1) who was separated from such service under honorable conditions,

(2) who is still in such service, or

(3) who has been retired, is entitled to receive compensation of ten dollars for each month during which such person was in active domestic service during the compensable period, fifteen dollars for each month during which such person was in active foreign service, but not Vietnam service, during the compensable period, and twenty dollars for each month during which such person was in active Vietnam service. The maximum amount of cash payable to any qualified applicant, unless such applicant qualifies for a payment based upon missing in action or prisoner of war status or unless such applicant qualifies for a survivor's payment, is five hundred dollars. No compensation shall be paid under this section to any person who received from another state a bonus or compensation of a like nature or to any person who has not served on active duty in the armed forces of the United States during the compensable period for at least ninety days unless active duty within such compensable period was terminated as a result of injuries or illness sustained in Vietnam service. Compensation for a fraction of a month of service shall be paid on the basis of one-thirtieth of the appropriate monthly amounts for each day of such service. Persons medically discharged or medically retired from service due to combat related disabilities sustained in Vietnam service shall be paid five hundred dollars. Service in the Merchant Marine of the United States shall not be considered for the purpose of this section. As used in this section "domestic service" means service within the territorial limits of the fifty states, excluding sea duty; "foreign service" means service in all other places, excluding Vietnam service; and "Vietnam service" means military service within the Republic of Vietnam during the period between February 28, 1961 through July 1, 1973 or military service in southeast Asia for which hostile fire pay was awarded pursuant to Title 37, Section 310, United States Code, during the period February 28, 1961 through July 1, 1973. No compensation shall be paid under this section to any person for any periods of time spent under penal confinement during the period of active duty. Either the surviving spouse, or the surviving child or children, or the surviving parents, including persons standing in loco parentis for one year preceding commencement of service in the armed forces of the United States, of a deceased person shall be paid the same amount of compensation that the deceased would have been entitled to receive under this section, if living. If such deceased person's death is determined by the Veterans Administration of the United States to have been the result of injuries or illness sustained in Vietnam service his survivors as herein designated, are entitled to one thousand dollars, regardless of the amount of compensation which the deceased would have been entitled to receive under this section, if living. The amount of compensation payable to such survivors shall be payable only to one of the three groups of survivors herein designated in the order in which said groups are named. Every person designated by the United States Department of Defense as missing in action as a result of honorable service or as held in enemy captivity or who is the spouse, or the child, or the parent, including persons standing in loco parentis for one year preceding commencement of service, of a person designated by the Department of Defense as missing in action as a result of honorable service or held in enemy captivity, is entitled to one thousand dollars in lieu of other cash benefits payable under this section. The amount of compensation payable to such claimants for such missing or captive person shall be payable only to one of the groups of claimants herein designated in the order in which said groups are named. No payment to any survivor of a person designated as missing in action as a result of honorable service or held in enemy captivity, while such person is held captive or is missing in action, shall prevent such missing or captive person from claiming and receiving a bonus of an equal amount upon his being released or located. The General Assembly shall provide by law for an educational assistance bonus which may be taken in lieu of the cash bonus by any person who served on active duty in the armed forces of the United States and who qualifies for a cash bonus under this section. The educational assistance bonus shall offer financial assistance at any educational institution deemed appropriate by the General Assembly. Such financial assistance shall be equal to twice the amount of the cash bonus for which such person qualifies under this section. No sale or assignment of any right or claim to compensation under this section shall be valid, no claims of creditors shall be enforceable against rights or claims to or payments of compensation under this section, and no fees shall be charged for services in connection with the prosecution of any right or claim to compensation or the collection of any compensation under this section. The commissioners shall have complete charge of making payments of the compensation provided for in this section and shall adopt and promulgate regulations governing their procedure in connection therewith, including determinations as to who are proper beneficiaries and the amounts to which such beneficiaries are entitled, determinations as to whether an applicant has the necessary residence requirements, and such other regulations that are necessary and proper. All applications for payment of compensation or educational bonuses under this section shall be made to the commissioners before January 1, 1978. The commissioners shall select and appoint such legal counsel and employees as are necessary, fix their compensation and prescribe their duties, and all such appointees shall serve at its pleasure. When practical, the commissioners shall employ Vietnam veterans to fill such positions. The commissioners shall permit review of individual records of claims by representatives of recognized veterans organizations when authorized to do so by the applicant. There is hereby transferred to the Vietnam Conflict Compensation Fund, for the purpose of defraying the immediate cost of administration and compensation, out of the funds known as the "Korean Conflict Compensation Fund" and the "Korean Conflict Compensation Bond Retirement Fund" created by Section 2d of Article VIII of the Ohio Constitution, the balance remaining after provision for payment of all outstanding bonds or notes, coupons, and charges. The people of this state declare it to be their intention to in no manner affect or change any of the existing provisions of the constitution except as herein set forth. The provisions of this section shall be self executing. Upon payment of all valid claims for cash compensation made within the limitations of time as prescribed herein, the commissioners may transfer any funds in the Vietnam Conflict Compensation Fund to the Vietnam Conflict Compensation Bond Retirement

Fund. Upon retirement of all of the bonds or notes that may be issued hereunder and the payment of all valid claims for cash compensation made within the limitations of time as prescribed herein, the commissioners of the sinking fund shall make a final report to the General Assembly, and any balance remaining in any of the funds herein created and referred to shall be disposed of as shall be provided by law.

Section 2k. Issuance of Bonds for Local Government Public Infrastructure Capital Improvements

(A) In addition to the authorization otherwise contained in Article VIII of the Ohio Constitution, the General Assembly may provide by law, in accordance with but subject to the limitations of this section, for the issuance of bonds and other obligations of the state for the purpose of financing or assisting in the financing of the cost of public infrastructure capital improvements of municipal corporations, counties, townships, and other governmental entities as designated by law. As used in this section public infrastructure capital improvements shall be limited to roads and bridges, waste water treatment systems, water supply systems, solid waste disposal facilities and storm water and sanitary collection, storage, and treatment facilities, including real property, interests in real property, facilities, and equipment related or incidental thereto. Capital improvements shall include without limitation the cost of acquisition, construction, reconstruction, expansion improvement, planning and equipping. It is hereby determined that such public infrastructure capital improvements are necessary to preserve and expand the public capital infrastructure of such municipal corporations, counties, townships, and other governmental entities, ensure the public health, safety, and welfare, create and preserve jobs, enhance employment opportunities, and improve the economic welfare of the people of this state.

(B)(1) Not more than one hundred twenty million dollars principal amount of bonds and other obligations authorized under this section may be issued in any calendar year, provided that the aggregate total principal amount of bonds and other obligations authorized and issued under this section may not exceed one billion two hundred million dollars. Further limitations may be provided by law upon the amount of bonds that may be issued under this section in any year in order that the total debt charges of the state shall not exceed a proportion of general revenue fund expenditures that would adversely affect the credit rating of the state. If obligations are issued under this section to retire or refund obligations previously issued under this section, the new obligations shall not be counted against those calendar year or total issuance limitations to the extent that their principal amount does not exceed the principal amount of the obligations to be retired or refunded.

(2) Provision shall be made by law for the use to the extent practicable of Ohio products, materials, services, and labor in the making of any project financed, in whole or in part, under this section.

(C) The state may participate in any public infrastructure capital improvement under this section with municipal corporations, counties, townships, or other governmental entities, or any one or more of them. Such participation may be by grants, loans, or contributions to them for any of such capital improvements. The entire proceeds of the bonds shall be used for the public infrastructure capital improvements of municipal corporations, counties, townships, and other governmental entities, except to the extent that the General Assembly provides by law that the state may be reasonably compensated from such moneys for planning, financial management, or other administrative services performed in relation to the bond issuance.

(D)(1) Each issue of obligations issued under this section shall mature in not more than thirty years from the date of issuance, or, if issued to retire or refund other obligations issued under this section, within thirty years from the date the debt was originally contracted. If obligations are issued as notes in anticipation of the issuance of bonds, provision shall be made by law for the establishment and maintenance, during the period in which the notes are outstanding, of a special fund or funds in to which shall be paid, from the sources authorized for the payment of such bonds, the amount that would have been sufficient, if bonds maturing during a period of thirty years had been issued without such prior issuance of notes, to pay the principal that would have been payable on such bonds during such period. Such fund or funds shall be used solely for the payment of principal of such notes or of bonds in anticipation of which such notes have been issued.

(2) The obligations issued under this section are general obligations of the state. The full faith and credit, revenue, and taxing power of the state shall be pledged to the payment of the principal of and interest on such obligations as they become due hereinafter called debt service, and bond retirement fund provisions shall be made for payment of debt service. Provision shall be made by law for the sufficiency and appropriation, for purposes of paying debt service, of excises, taxes, and revenues so pledged to debt service, and for covenants to continue the levy, collection and application of sufficient excises, taxes, and revenues to the extent needed for such purpose.
Notwithstanding Section 22 of Article II, Ohio Constitution, no further act of appropriation shall be necessary for that purpose. The obligations and the provision for the payment of debt service and repayment of any loans hereunder by governmental entities are not subject to Sections 5, 6, and 11 of Article XII Ohio Constitution.

(3) The moneys referred to in Section 5a of Article XII, Ohio Constitution, may not be pledged to the payment of debt service on obligations issued under authority of this section.

(4) The obligations issued under authority of this section, the transfer thereof, and the interest and other income therefrom, including any profit made on the sale thereof, shall at all times be free from taxation within the state.

(E) This section shall otherwise be implemented in the manner and to the extent provided by law by the General Assembly.

Section 2l. Parks, Recreation, and Natural Resources Project Capital Improvements

(A) In addition to the authorizations otherwise contained in Article VIII of the Ohio Constitution, the General Assembly shall provide by law, in accordance with and subject to the limitations of this section, for the issuance of bonds and other obligations of the state for the purpose of financing or assisting in the financing of the costs of capital improvements for state and local parks and land and water recreation facilities; soil and water restoration and protection, land management including preservation of natural areas and reforestation; water management including dam safety, stream and lake management, and flood control and flood damage reduction, fish and wildlife resource management; and other projects that enhance the use and enjoyment of natural resources by individuals. Capital improvements include without limitation the cost of acquisition, construction, reconstruction, expansion, improvement, planning, and equipping. It is hereby determined that these capital improvements and provisions for them are necessary and appropriate to improve the quality of life of the people of this state, to better ensure the public health, safety, and welfare, and to create and preserve jobs and enhance employment opportunities.

(B)(1) Not more than fifty million dollars principal amount of obligations may be issued under this section in any fiscal year, and not more than two hundred million dollars principal amount may be outstanding at any one time. The limitations of this paragraph do not apply to any obligations authorized to be issued under this section to retire or refund obligations previously issued under this section, to the extent that their principal amount does not exceed the principal amount of the obligations to be retired or refunded.

(2) Each issue of obligations shall mature in not more than twenty-five years from the date of issuance, or, if issued to retire or refund other obligations issued under this section, within twenty-five years from the date the debt was originally contracted. If obligations are issued as bond anticipation notes, provision shall be made, by law or in the proceedings for the issuance of those notes, for the establishment and maintenance while the notes are outstanding of a special fund or funds into which there shall be paid, from the sources authorized for the payment of the bonds, the amount that would have been sufficient, if bonds maturing serially in each year over a period of twenty-five years had been issued without the prior issuance of the notes, to pay the principal that would have been payable on those bonds during that period; such fund or funds shall be used solely for the payment of principal of those notes or of the bonds anticipated.

(C) The state may participate by grants or contributions in financing capital improvements under this section made by local government entities. Of the proceeds of the first two hundred million dollars principal amount in obligations issued under this section for capital improvements, at least twenty per cent shall be allocated to grants or contributions to local government entities for such capital improvements.

(D) The obligations issued under this section are general obligations of the state. The full faith and credit, revenue, and taxing power of the state shall be pledged to the payment of the principal of and interest and other accreted amounts on those obligations as they become due, and bond retirement fund provisions shall be made for payment of that debt service. Provision shall be made by law for the sufficiency and appropriation for purposes of paying that debt service, of excises, taxes, and revenues so pledged to that debt service, and for covenants to continue the levy, collection, and application of sufficient excises, taxes, and revenues to the extent needed for that purpose. Notwithstanding Section 22 of Article II, Ohio Constitution, no further act of appropriation shall be necessary for that purpose. The moneys referred to in Section 5a of Article XII, Ohio Constitution, may not be pledged to the payment of that debt service. The obligations and the provisions for the payment of debt service on them are not subject to Sections 5, 6, and 11 of Article XII Ohio Constitution, and, with respect to the purposes to which their proceeds are to be applied, are not subject to Sections 4 and 6 of Article VIII, Ohio Constitution.

(E) Obligations issued under authority of this section, the transfer thereof, and the interest and other income and accreted amounts therefrom including any profit made on the sale thereof, shall at all times be free from taxation within the state.

(F) This section shall be implemented in the manner and to the extent provided by law by the General Assembly.

Section 2m. Issuance of General Obligations

(A) In addition to the authorizations otherwise contained in Article VIII of the Ohio Constitution, the general assembly may provide by law, in accordance with but subject to the limitations of this section, for the issuance of bonds and other obligations of the state for the purpose of financing or assisting in the financing of the cost of public infrastructure capital improvements of municipal corporations, counties, townships, and other governmental entities as designated by law, and the cost of highway capital improvements. As used in this section, public infrastructure capital improvements shall be limited to roads and bridges, waste water treatment systems, water supply systems, solid waste disposal facilities, and storm water and sanitary collection, storage, and treatment facilities, including real property, interests in real property, facilities, and equipment related to or incidental thereto, and shall include without limitation the cost of acquisition, construction, reconstruction, expansion, improvement, planning, and equipping. As used in this section, highway capital improvements shall be limited to highways, including those on the state highway system and urban extensions thereof, those within or leading to public parks or recreation areas, and those within or leading to municipal corporations, and shall include without limitation the cost of acquisition, construction, reconstruction, expansion, improvement, planning, and equipping. It is hereby determined that such public infrastructure capital improvements and highway capital improvements are necessary to preserve and expand the public capital infrastructure of the state and its municipal corporations, counties, townships, and other governmental entities, ensure the public health, safety, and welfare, create and preserve jobs, enhance employment opportunities, and improve the economic welfare of the people of this state.

(B) Not more than one hundred twenty million dollars principal amount of the infrastructure obligations authorized to be issued under this section, plus the principal amount of infrastructure obligations that in any prior fiscal years could have been but were not issued within the one-hundred-twenty-million-dollar fiscal year limit, may be issued in any fiscal year, provided that the aggregate total principal amount of infrastructure obligations issued under this section for public infrastructure capital improvements may not exceed one billion two hundred million dollars; and provided further that no infrastructure obligations shall be issued pursuant to this section until at least one billion one hundred ninety-nine million five hundred thousand dollars aggregate principal amount of obligations have been issued pursuant to section 2k of Article VIII. Not more than two hundred twenty million dollars principal amount of highway obligations authorized to be issued under this section, plus the principal amount of highway obligations that in any prior fiscal years could have been but were not issued within the two-hundred- twenty-million-dollar fiscal year limit, may be issued in any fiscal year, and not more than one billion two hundred million dollars principal amount of highway obligations issued under this section may be outstanding at any one time. Further limitations may be provided by law upon the amount of infrastructure obligations and highway obligations, hereinafter collectively called obligations, that may be issued under this section in any fiscal year in order that the total debt charges of the state payable from the general revenue fund shall not exceed a proportion of general revenue fund expenditures that would adversely affect the credit rating of the state. If obligations are issued under this section to retire or refund obligations previously issued under this section, the new obligations shall not be counted against those fiscal year or total issuance limitations to the extent that their principal amount does not exceed the principal amount of the obligations to be retired or refunded. Provision shall be made by law for the use to the extent practicable of Ohio products, materials, services, and labor in the making of any project financed, in whole or in part, under this section.

(C) The state may participate in any public infrastructure capital improvement or highway capital improvement under this section with municipal corporations, counties, townships, or other governmental entities as designated by law, or any one or more of them. Such participation may be by grants, loans, or contributions to them for any such capital improvements. The entire proceeds of the infrastructure obligations shall be used for public infrastructure capital improvements of municipal corporations, counties, townships, and other governmental entities, except to the extent that the general assembly provides by law that the state may reasonably be compensated from such moneys for planning, financial management, or administrative services performed in relation to the issuance of infrastructure obligations.

(D) Each issue of obligations shall mature in not more than thirty years from the date of issuance, or, if issued to retire or refund other obligations, within thirty years from the date the debt originally was contracted. If obligations are issued as notes in anticipation of the issuance of bonds, provision shall be made by law for the establishment and maintenance, during the period in which the notes are outstanding, of a special fund or funds into which shall be paid, from the sources authorized for the payment of such bonds, the amount that would have been sufficient, if bonds maturing during a period of thirty years had been issued without such prior issuance of notes, to pay the principal that would have been payable on such bonds during such period. Such fund or funds shall be used solely for the payment of principal of such notes or bonds in anticipation of which such notes have been issued. The obligations are general obligations of the state. The full faith and credit, revenue, and taxing power of the state shall be pledged to the payment of the principal of and premium and interest and other accreted amounts on outstanding obligations as they become due, hereinafter called debt service, and bond retirement fund provisions shall be made for payment of debt service. Provision shall be made by law for the sufficiency and appropriation, for purposes of paying debt service, of excises, taxes, and revenues so pledged to debt service, and for covenants to continue the levy, collection, and application of sufficient excises, taxes, and revenues to the extent needed for such purpose. Notwithstanding Section 22 of Article II, Ohio Constitution, no further act of appropriation shall be necessary for that purpose. The obligations and the provision for the payment of debt service, and repayment by governmental entities of any loans made under this section are not subject to Sections 5, 6, and 11 of Article XII, Ohio Constitution. The moneys referred to in Section 5a of Article XII, Ohio Constitution may be pledged to the payment of debt service on highway obligations, but may not be pledged to the payment of debt service on infrastructure obligations. In each year that moneys referred to in Section 5a of Article XII, Ohio Constitution pledged to the payment of debt service on highway obligations issued under this section are available for such purpose, such moneys shall be appropriated thereto and the required application of any other excises and taxes shall be reduced in corresponding amount. The obligations issued under authority of this section, the transfer thereof, and the interest, interest equivalent, and other income and accreted amounts therefrom, including any profit made on the sale, exchange, or other disposition thereof, shall at all times be free from taxation within the state.

(E) This section shall otherwise be implemented in the manner and to the extent provided by law by the general assembly, including provision for the procedure for incurring and issuing obligations, separately or in combination with other state obligations, and refunding, retiring, and evidencing obligations.

(F) The authorizations in this section are in addition to authorizations contained in other sections of Article VIII, Ohio Constitution, are in addition to and not a limitation upon the authority of the general assembly under other provisions of this constitution, and do not impair any law previously enacted by the general assembly, except that after December 31, 1996, no additional highway obligations of the state may be issued for any highway purposes under Section 2i of Article VIII, Ohio Constitution, except to refund highway obligations issued under section 2i that are outstanding on that date.

Section 2n. Facilities for System of Common Schools and Facilities for State-Supported and State-Assisted Institutions of Higher Education

(A) The General Assembly may provide by law, subject to the limitations of and in accordance with this section, for the issuance of bonds and other obligations of the state for the purpose of paying costs of facilities for a system of common schools throughout the state and facilities for state-supported and state-assisted institutions of higher education. As used in this section, "costs" includes, without limitation, the costs of acquisition, construction, improvement, expansion, planning, and equipping.

(B) Each obligation issued under this section shall mature no later than the thirty-first day of December of the twenty-fifth calendar year after its issuance except that obligations issued to refund other obligations shall mature not later than the thirty-first day of December of the twenty-fifth calendar year after the year in which the original obligation to pay was issued or entered into.

(C) Obligations issued under this section are general obligations of the state. The full faith and credit, revenue, and taxing power of the state shall be pledged to the payment of debt service on those outstanding obligations as it becomes due. For purposes of the full and timely payment of that debt service, appropriate provisions shall be made or authorized by law for bond retirement funds, for the sufficiency and appropriation of excises, taxes, and revenues so pledged to that debt service, for which purpose, notwithstanding Section 22 of Article II of the Ohio Constitution, no further act of appropriation shall be necessary, and for covenants to continue the levy, collection, and application of sufficient excises, taxes, and revenues to the extent needed for that purpose. Those obligations and the provisions for the payment of debt service on them are not subject to Sections 5, 6, and 11 of Article XII of the Ohio Constitution. Moneys referred to in Section 5a of Article XII of the Ohio Constitution may not be pledged or used for the payment of the debt service on those obligations. Moneys consisting of net state lottery proceeds may be pledged or used for payment of debt service on obligations issued under this section to pay costs of facilities for a system of common schools, but not on obligations issued under this section to pay costs of facilities for state-supported and state-assisted institutions of higher education. In the case of the issuance of any of those obligations as bond anticipation notes, provision shall be made by law or in the bond or note proceedings for the establishment and the maintenance, during the period the notes are outstanding, of special funds into which there shall be paid, from the sources authorized for payment of the bonds anticipated, the amount that would have been sufficient to pay the principal that would have been payable on those bonds during that period if bonds maturing serially in each year over the maximum period of maturity referred to in division (B) of this section had been issued without the prior issuance of the notes. Those special funds and investment income on them shall be used solely for the payment of principal of those notes or of the bonds anticipated.

(D) As used in this section, "debt service" means principal and interest and other accreted amounts payable on the obligations referred to.

(E) Obligations issued under this section, their transfer, and the interest, interest equivalent, and other income or accreted amounts on them, including any profit made on their sale, exchange, or other disposition, shall at all times be free from taxation within the state.

(F) This section shall be implemented in the manner and to the extent provided by the General Assembly by law, including provision for the procedure for incurring, refunding, retiring, and evidencing obligations issued as referred to in this section. The total principal amount of obligations issued under this section shall be as determined by the General Assembly, subject to the limitation provided for in Section 17 of this article.

(G) The authorizations in this section are in addition to authorizations contained in other sections of this article, are in addition to and not a limitation upon the authority of the General Assembly under other provisions of this Constitution, and do not impair any law previously enacted by the General Assembly.

Section 2o. Issuance of Bonds and Other Obligations for Environmental Conservation and Revitalization Purposes

(A) It is determined and confirmed that the environmental and related conservation, preservation, and revitalization purposes referred to in divisions (A)(1) and (2) of this section, and provisions for them, are proper public purposes of the state and local governmental entities and are necessary and appropriate means to improve the quality of life and the general and economic well-being of the people of this state; to better ensure the public health, safety, and welfare; to protect water and other natural resources; to provide for the conservation and preservation of natural and open areas and farmlands, including by making urban areas more desirable or suitable for development and revitalization; to control, prevent, minimize, clean up, or remediate certain contamination of or pollution from lands in the state and water contamination or pollution; to provide for safe and productive urban land use or reuse; to enhance the availability, public use, and enjoyment of natural areas and resources; and to create and preserve jobs and enhance employment opportunities. Those purposes are:

(1) Conservation purposes, meaning conservation and preservation of natural areas, open spaces, and farmlands and other lands devoted to agriculture, including by acquiring land or interests therein; provision of state and local park and recreation facilities, and other actions that permit and enhance the availability, public use, and enjoyment of natural areas and open spaces in Ohio; and land, forest, water, and other natural resource management projects;

(2) Revitalization purposes, meaning providing for and enabling the environmentally safe and productive development and use or reuse of publicly and privately owned lands, including those within urban areas, by the remediation or clean up, or planning and assessment for remediation or clean up, of contamination, or addressing, by clearance, land acquisition or assembly, infrastructure, or otherwise, that or other property conditions or circumstances that may be deleterious to the public health and safety and the environment and water and other natural resources, or that preclude or inhibit environmentally sound or economic use or reuse of the property.

(B) The General Assembly may provide by law, subject to the limitations of and in accordance with this section, for the issuance of bonds and other obligations of the state for the purpose of paying costs of projects implementing those purposes.

(1) Not more than two hundred million dollars principal amount of obligations issued under this section for conservation purposes may be outstanding in accordance with their terms at any one time. Not more than fifty million dollars principal amount of those obligations, plus the principal amount of those obligations that in any prior fiscal year could have been but were not issued within the fifty-million-dollar fiscal year limit, may be issued in any fiscal year. Those obligations shall be general obligations of the state and the full faith and credit, revenue, and taxing power of the state shall be pledged to the payment of debt service on them as it becomes due, all as provided in this section.

(2) Not more than two hundred million dollars principal amount of obligations issued under this section for revitalization purposes may be outstanding in accordance with their terms at any one time. Not more than fifty million dollars principal amount of those obligations, plus the principal amount of those obligations that in any prior fiscal year could have been but were not issued within the fifty-million-dollar fiscal year limit, may be issued in any fiscal year. Those obligations shall not be general obligations of the state and the full faith and credit, revenue, and taxing power of the state shall not be pledged to the payment of debt service on them. Those obligations shall be secured by a pledge of all or such portion of designated revenues and receipts of the state as the General Assembly authorizes, including receipts from designated taxes or excises, other state revenues from sources other than state taxes or excises, such as from state enterprise activities, and payments for or related to those revitalization purposes made by or on behalf of local governmental entities, responsible parties, or others. The General Assembly shall provide by law for prohibitions or restrictions on the granting or lending of proceeds of obligations issued under division (B)(2) of this section to parties to pay costs of cleanup or remediation of contamination for which they are determined to be responsible.

(C) For purposes of the full and timely payment of debt service on state obligations authorized by this section, appropriate provision shall be made or authorized by law for bond retirement funds, for the sufficiency and appropriation of state excises, taxes, and revenues pledged to the debt service on the respective obligations, for which purpose, notwithstanding Section 22 of Article II of the Ohio Constitution, no further act of appropriation shall be necessary, and for covenants to continue the levy, collection, and application of sufficient state excises, taxes, and revenues to the extent needed for those purposes. Moneys referred to in Section 5a of Article XII of the Ohio Constitution may not be pledged or used for the payment of debt service on those obligations. As used in this section, "debt service" means principal and interest and other accreted amounts payable on the obligations referred to.

(D)(1) Divisions (B) and (C) of this section shall be implemented in the manner and to the extent provided by the General Assembly by law, including provision for procedures for incurring, refunding, retiring, and evidencing state obligations issued pursuant to this section. Each state obligation issued pursuant to this section shall mature no later than the thirty-first day of December of the twenty-fifth calendar year after its issuance, except that obligations issued to refund or retire other obligations shall mature not later than the thirty-first day of December of the twenty-fifth calendar year after the year in which the original obligation to pay was issued or entered into.

(2) In the case of the issuance of state obligations under this section as bond anticipation notes, provision shall be made by law or in the bond or note proceedings for the establishment, and the maintenance during the period the notes are outstanding, of special funds into which there shall be paid, from the sources authorized for payment of the particular bonds anticipated, the amount that would have been sufficient to pay the principal that would have been payable on those bonds during that period if bonds maturing serially in each year over the maximum period of maturity referred to in division (D)(1) of this section had been issued without the prior issuance of the notes. Those special funds and investment income on them shall be used solely for the payment of principal of those notes or of the bonds anticipated.

(E) In addition to projects undertaken by the state, the state may participate or assist, by grants, loans, loan guarantees, or contributions, in the financing of projects for purposes referred to in this section that are undertaken by local governmental entities or by others, including, but not limited to, not-for-profit organizations, at the direction or authorization of local governmental entities. Obligations of the state issued under this section and the provisions for payment of debt service on them, including any payments by local governmental entities, are not subject to Sections 6 and 11 of Article XII of the Ohio Constitution. Those obligations, and obligations of local governmental entities issued for the public purposes referred to in this section, and provisions for payment of debt service on them, and the purposes and uses to which the proceeds of those state or local obligations, or moneys from other sources, are to be or may be applied, are not subject to Sections 4 and 6 of Article VIII of the Ohio Constitution.

(F) The powers and authority granted or confirmed by and under this section, and the determinations and confirmations in this section, are independent of, in addition to, and not in derogation of or a limitation on, powers, authority, determinations, or confirmations under laws, charters, ordinances, or resolutions, or by or under other provisions of the Ohio Constitution including, without limitation, Section 36 of Article II, Sections 2i, 2l, 2m, and 13 of Article VIII, and Articles X and XVIII, and do not impair any previously adopted provision of the Ohio Constitution or any law previously enacted by the General Assembly.

(G) Obligations issued under this section, their transfer, and the interest, interest equivalent, and other income or accreted amounts on them, including any profit made on their sale, exchange, or other disposition, shall at all times be free from taxation within the state.

Section 2p. Issuance of Bonds for Economic and Educational Purposes and Local Government Projects

(A) It is determined and confirmed that the development purposes referred to in this division, and provisions for them, are proper public purposes of the state and local governmental entities and are necessary and appropriate means to create and preserve jobs and enhance employment and educational opportunities; to improve the quality of life and the general and economic well-being of all the people and businesses in all areas of this state, including economically disadvantaged businesses and individuals; and to preserve and expand the public capital infrastructure; all to better ensure the public health, safety, and welfare. Those purposes are:

(1) Public infrastructure capital improvements, which shall be limited to roads and bridges, waste water treatment systems, water supply systems, solid waste disposal facilities, and storm water and sanitary collection, storage, and treatment facilities, including real property, interests in real property, facilities, and equipment related to or incidental thereto, and shall include, without limitation, the cost of acquisition, construction, reconstruction, expansion, improvement, planning, and equipping;

(2) Research and development in support of Ohio industry, commerce, and business (hereinafter referred to as "research and development purposes"), which shall include, without limitation, research and product innovation, development, and commercialization through efforts by and collaboration among Ohio business and industry, state and local public entities and agencies, public and private education institutions, or research organizations and institutions, all as may be further provided for by state or local law, but excluding purposes provided for in Section 15 of Article VIII, Ohio Constitution; and

(3) Development of sites and facilities in Ohio for and in support of industry, commerce, distribution, and research and development purposes.

(B) The General Assembly may provide by law, in accordance with but subject to the limitations of this section, for the issuance of general obligation bonds and other obligations of the state for the purpose of financing or assisting in the financing of the cost of projects implementing those purposes.

(1) Not more than one billion three hundred fifty million dollars principal amount of state general obligations may be issued under this section for public infrastructure capital improvements. Not more than one hundred twenty million dollars principal amount of those obligations may be issued in each of the first five fiscal years of issuance and not more than one hundred fifty million dollars principal amount of those obligations may be issued in each of the next five fiscal years of issuance, plus in each case the principal amount of those obligations that in any prior fiscal year could have been but were not issued within those fiscal year limits. No infrastructure obligations may be issued pursuant to this division and division (C) of this section until at least one billion one hundred ninety-nine million five hundred thousand dollars aggregate principal amount of state infrastructure obligations have been issued pursuant to Section 2m of Article VIII, Ohio Constitution.

(2) Not more than one billion two hundred million dollars principal amount of state general obligations may be issued under this section for research and development purposes. Not more than four hundred fifty million dollars principal amount of those obligations may be issued in total from fiscal years 2006 through 2011, not more than two hundred twenty-five million dollars principal amount of those obligations may be issued in the next fiscal year of issuance, and not more than one hundred seventy-five million dollars principal amount of those obligations may be issued in any other fiscal year, plus in each case the principal amount of those obligations that in any prior fiscal year could have been but were not issued.

(3) Not more than one hundred fifty million dollars principal amount of state general obligations may be issued under this section for development of sites and facilities for industry, commerce, distribution, and research and development purposes. Not more than thirty million dollars principal amount of those obligations may be issued in each of the first three fiscal years of issuance, and not more than fifteen million dollars principal amount of those obligations may be issued in any other fiscal year, plus in each case the principal amount of those obligations that in any prior fiscal year could have been but were not issued.

(C) Each issue of state general obligations for public infrastructure capital improvements or development of sites and facilities shall mature in not more than thirty years from the date of issuance, and each issue of state general obligations for research and development purposes shall mature in not more than twenty years from the date of issuance; or, if issued to retire or refund other obligations, within that number of years from the date the debt being retired or refunded was originally issued. If state general obligations are issued as notes in anticipation of the issuance of bonds, provision shall be made by law for the establishment and maintenance, during the period in which the notes are outstanding, of a special fund or funds into which shall be paid, from the sources authorized for the payment of such bonds, the amount that would have been sufficient, if bonds maturing during the permitted period of years had been issued without such prior issuance of notes, to pay the principal that would have been payable on such bonds during such period. Such fund or funds shall be used solely for the payment of principal of such notes or bonds in anticipation of which such notes have been issued. Notwithstanding anything to the contrary in Section 2k or 2m of Article VIII, obligations issued under this section or Section 2k or 2m to retire or refund obligations previously issued under this section or Section 2k or 2m shall not be counted against the fiscal year or total issuance limitations provided in this section or Section 2k or 2m, as applicable.

The obligations issued under this division and division (B) of this section are general obligations of the state. The full faith and credit, revenue, and taxing power of the state shall be pledged to the payment of the principal of and premium and interest and other accreted amounts on outstanding obligations as they become due (hereinafter called debt service), and bond retirement fund provisions shall be made for payment of that debt service. Provision shall be made by law for the sufficiency and appropriation, for purposes of paying debt service, of excises, taxes, and revenues so pledged or committed to debt service, and for covenants to continue the levy, collection, and application of sufficient excises, taxes, and revenues to the extent needed for that purpose. Notwithstanding Section 22 of Article II, Ohio Constitution, no further act of appropriation shall be necessary for that purpose. The obligations and the provision for the payment of debt service, and repayment by governmental entities of any loans made under this section, are not subject to Sections 5, 6, and 11 of Article XII, Ohio Constitution. Moneys referred to in Section 5a of Article XII, Ohio Constitution may not be pledged or used for the payment of that debt service. Debt service on obligations issued for research and development purposes and for development of sites and facilities shall not be included in the calculation of total debt service for purposes of division (A) of Section 17 of Article VIII, Ohio Constitution.

(D)(1) The state may participate in any public infrastructure capital improvement under this section with municipal corporations, counties, townships, or other governmental entities as designated by law, or any one or more of them. Such participation may be by grants, loans, or contributions to them for any such capital improvements. The entire proceeds of the infrastructure obligations shall be used for public infrastructure capital improvements of municipal corporations, counties, townships, and other governmental entities, except to the extent that the General Assembly provides by law that the state may reasonably be compensated from such moneys for planning, financial management, or administrative services performed in relation to the issuance of infrastructure obligations.

(2)(a) Implementation of the research and development purposes includes supporting any and all related matters and activities, including: attracting researchers and research teams by endowing research chairs or otherwise; activities to develop and commercialize products and processes; intellectual property matters such as copyrights and patents; property interests, including time sharing arrangements; and financial rights and matters such as royalties, licensing, and other financial gain or sharing resulting from research and development purposes. State and local public moneys, including the proceeds of bonds, notes, and other obligations, may be used to pay costs of or in support of or related to these research and development purposes, including, without limitation, capital formation, direct operating costs, costs of research and facilities, including interests in real property therefore, and support for public and private institutions of higher education, research organizations or institutions, and private sector entities. The exercise of these powers by the state and state agencies, including state-supported and state-assisted institutions of higher education, and local public entities and agencies, may be jointly or in coordination with each other, with researchers or research organizations and institutions, with private institutions of higher education, with individuals, or with private sector entities. State and local public participation may be in such manner as the entity or agency determines, including by any one or a combination of grants, loans including loans to lenders or the purchase of loans, subsidies, contributions, advances, or guarantees, or by direct investments of or payment or reimbursement from available moneys, or by providing staffing or other support, including computer or other technology capacity, or equipment or facilities, including interests in real property therefore, and either alone or jointly, in collaborative or cooperative ventures, with other public agencies and private sector entities including not for profit entities. In addition to other state-level monetary participation as referred to in this section or otherwise, state-supported and state-assisted institutions of higher education may, as authorized from time to time by the General Assembly, issue obligations to pay costs of participating in and implementing research and development purposes. In addition to the other obligations authorized in or pursuant to this section, the General Assembly also may authorize the state and state agencies and local public entities and agencies, and corporations not for profit designated by any of them as such agencies or instrumentalities, to issue obligations to borrow and loan or otherwise provide moneys for research and development purposes, including, but not limited to, obligations for which moneys raised by taxation shall not be obligated or pledged for the payment of debt service and which are therefore not subject to Sections 5, 6, and 11 of Article XII, Ohio Constitution.

(b) Implementation of the research and development purposes shall include utilization of independent reviewers to review the merits of proposed research and development projects and to make recommendations concerning which proposed projects should be awarded support from the proceeds of the sale of obligations under this section. Prior to the utilization of an independent reviewer, the state agency proposing to award the support for a project shall provide the name and other descriptive information regarding the independent reviewer to the Governor, the President and Minority Leader of the Senate, and the Speaker and Minority Leader of the House of Representatives. If the recommendations of an independent reviewer with respect to a proposed project are not adopted by the state agency proposing to award the support for the project, the agency shall notify the Governor, the President and Minority Leader of the Senate, and the Speaker and Minority Leader of the House of Representatives of that fact and explain the reasons for not adopting the recommendations.

(c) From the proceeds of the sale of obligations issued under this section, not more than four hundred fifty million dollars may be awarded, promised, or otherwise committed in total for research and development purposes from fiscal years 2006 through 2011, not more than two hundred twenty-five million dollars may be awarded, promised, or otherwise committed for research and development purposes in fiscal year 2012, and not more than one hundred seventy-five million dollars may be awarded, promised, or otherwise committed for research and development purposes in any other fiscal year beginning in fiscal year 2013 and thereafter, plus in each case the amount of the proceeds that in any prior fiscal year could have been but were not awarded.

(3) Development of sites and facilities for and in support of industry, commerce, distribution, and research and development purposes includes acquisition of real estate and interests in real estate, site preparation including any necessary remediation and cleanup, constructing and improving facilities, and providing public infrastructure capital improvements and other transportation and communications infrastructure improvements for and in support of the use of those sites and facilities for those purposes. State and local public moneys, including the proceeds of bonds, notes, and other obligations, may be used to pay costs of those purposes. The exercise of these powers by the state and state agencies and local public entities and agencies, may be jointly or in coordination with each other, and with individuals or private sector business entities. State and local public participation may be in such manner as the entity or agency determines, including by any one or a combination of grants, loans including loans to lenders or the purchase of loans, subsidies, contributions, advances, or guarantees, or by direct investments of or payment or reimbursement from available moneys. In addition to other state-level monetary participation as referred to in this section or otherwise, state-supported and state-assisted institutions of higher education, and local public entities and agencies may, as authorized from time to time by the General Assembly, issue obligations to pay costs of participating in and implementing the development of sites and facilities.

(E) Obligations issued under authority of this section for research and development purposes and site and facility development purposes, provisions for the payment of debt service on them, the purposes and uses to which and the manner in which the proceeds of those obligations or moneys from other sources are to or may be applied, and other implementation of those development purposes as referred to in this section, are not subject to Sections 4 and 6 of Article VIII, Ohio Constitution. Obligations issued under authority of this section, the transfer thereof, and the interest, interest equivalent, and other income and accreted amounts therefrom, including any profit made on the sale, exchange, or other disposition thereof, shall at all times be free from taxation within the state.

(F) This section shall otherwise be implemented in the manner and to the extent provided by law by the General Assembly, including provision for the procedure for incurring and issuing obligations, separately or in combination with other obligations, and refunding, retiring, and evidencing obligations; provision for ensuring the accountability of all state funding provided for the development purposes referred to in division (A) of this section; provision for restricting or limiting the taking of private property under Section 19 of Article I for disposition to private sector entities for the purposes identified in divisions (A)(2) and (3) of this section or restricting the disposition of that property to private sector entities or individuals;and provision for the implementation of the development purposes referred to in division (A) of this section to benefit people and businesses otherwise qualified for receipt of funding for the development purposes referred to in division (A) of this section, including economically disadvantaged businesses and individuals in all areas of this state, including by the use to the extent practicable of Ohio products, materials, services, and labor.

(G) The powers and authority granted or confirmed by and under, and the determinations in, this section are independent of, in addition to, and not in derogation of or a limitation on, powers, authority, determinations, or confirmations under laws or under other provisions of the Ohio Constitution including, without limitation, Section 7 of Article I, Section 5 of Article VI, Sections 2i, 2n, 2o, 13, and 15 of Article VIII, Article X, and Section 3 of Article XVIII, and do not impair any previously adopted provisions of the Ohio Constitution or any law previously enacted by the General Assembly or by a local public agency.

Section 2q. Issuance of Bonds for Continuation of Environmental Revitalization and Conservation

(A) It is determined and confirmed that the environmental and related conservation, preservation, and revitalization purposes referred to in divisions (A)(1) and (2) of this section, and provisions for them, are proper public purposes of the state and local governmental entities and are necessary and appropriate means to improve the quality of life and the general and economic well-being of the people of this state; to better ensure the public health, safety, and welfare; to protect water and other natural resources; to provide for the conservation and preservation of natural and open areas and farmlands, including by making urban areas more desirable or suitable for development and revitalization; to control, prevent, minimize, clean up, or remediate certain contamination of or pollution from lands in the state and water contamination or pollution; to provide for safe and productive urban land use or reuse; to enhance the availability, public use, and enjoyment of natural areas and resources; and to create and preserve jobs and enhance employment opportunities. Those purposes are:

(1) Conservation purposes, meaning conservation and preservation of natural areas, open spaces, and farmlands and other lands devoted to agriculture, including by acquiring land or interests therein; provision of state and local park and recreation facilities, and other actions that permit and enhance the availability, public use, and enjoyment of natural areas and open spaces in Ohio; and land, forest, water, and other natural resource management projects;

(2) Revitalization purposes, meaning providing for and enabling the environmentally safe and productive development and use or reuse of publicly and privately owned lands, including those within urban areas, by the remediation or clean up, or planning and assessment for remediation or clean up, of contamination, or addressing, by clearance, land acquisition or assembly, infrastructure, or otherwise, that or other property conditions or circumstances that may be deleterious to the public health and safety and the environment and water and other natural resources, or that preclude or inhibit environmentally sound or economic use or reuse of the property.

(B) The General Assembly may provide by law, subject to the limitations of and in accordance with this section, for the issuance of bonds and other obligations of the state for the purpose of paying costs of projects implementing those purposes.

(1) Not more than two hundred million dollars principal amount of obligations issued under this section for conservation purposes may be outstanding in accordance with their terms at any one time. Not more than fifty million dollars principal amount of those obligations, plus the principal amount of those obligations that in any prior fiscal year could have been but were not issued within the fifty-million dollar fiscal year limit, may be issued in any fiscal year. Those obligations shall be general obligations of the state and the full faith and credit, revenue, and taxing power of the state shall be pledged to the payment of debt service on them as it becomes due, all as provided in this section.

(2) Not more than two hundred million dollars principal amount of obligations issued under this section for revitalization purposes may be outstanding in accordance with their terms at any one time. Not more than fifty million dollars principal amount of those obligations, plus the principal amount of those obligations that in any prior fiscal year could have been but were not issued within the fifty-million-dollar fiscal year limit, may be issued in any fiscal year. Those obligations shall not be general obligations of the state and the full faith and credit, revenue, and taxing power of the state shall not be pledged to the payment of debt service on them. Those obligations shall be secured by a pledge of all or such portion of designated revenues and receipts of the state as the General Assembly authorizes, including receipts from designated taxes or excises, other state revenues from sources other than state taxes or excises, such as from state enterprise activities, and payments for or related to those revitalization purposes made by or on behalf of local governmental entities, responsible parties, or others. The general assembly shall provide by law for prohibitions or restrictions on the granting or lending of proceeds of obligations issued under division (B) (2) of this section to parties to pay costs of cleanup or remediation of contamination for which they are determined to be responsible.

(C) For purposes of the full and timely payment of debt service on state obligations authorized by this section, appropriate provision shall be made or authorized by law for bond retirement funds, for the sufficiency and appropriation of state excises, taxes, and revenues pledged to the debt service on the respective obligations, for which purpose, notwithstanding Section 22 of Article II of the Ohio Constitution, no further act of appropriation shall be necessary, and for covenants to continue the levy, collection, and application of sufficient state excises, taxes, and revenues to the extent needed for those purposes. Moneys referred to in Section 5a of Article XII of the Ohio Constitution may not be pledged or used for the payment of debt service on those obligations. As used in this section, "debt service" means principal and interest and other accreted amounts payable on the obligations referred to.

(D)(1) Divisions (B) and (C) of this section shall be implemented in the manner and to the extent provided by the General Assembly by law, including provision for procedures for incurring, refunding, retiring, and evidencing state obligations issued pursuant to this section. Each state obligation issued pursuant to this section shall mature no later than the thirty-first day of December of the twenty-fifth calendar year after its issuance, except that obligations issued to refund or retire other obligations shall mature not later than the thirty-first day of December of the twenty-fifth calendar year after the year in which the original obligation to pay was issued or entered into.

(2) In the case of the issuance of state obligations under this section as bond anticipation notes, provision shall be made by law or in the bond or note proceedings for the establishment, and the maintenance during the period the notes are outstanding, of special funds into which there shall be paid, from the sources authorized for payment of the particular bonds anticipated, the amount that would have been sufficient to pay the principal that would have been payable on those bonds during that period if bonds maturing serially in each year over the maximum period of maturity referred to in division (D)(1) of this section had been issued without the prior issuance of the notes. Those special funds and investment income on them shall be used solely for the payment of principal of those notes or of the bonds anticipated.

(E) In addition to projects undertaken by the state, the state may participate or assist, by grants, loans, loan guarantees, or contributions, in the financing of projects for purposes referred to in this section that are undertaken by local governmental entities or by others, including, but not limited to, not-forprofit organizations, at the direction or authorization of local governmental entities. Obligations of the state issued under this section and the provisions for payment of debt service on them, including any payments by local governmental entities, are not subject to Sections 6 and 11 of Article XII of the Ohio Constitution. Those obligations, and obligations of local governmental entities issued for the public purposes referred to in this section, and provisions for payment of debt service on them, and the purposes and uses to which the proceeds of those state or local obligations, or moneys from other sources, are to be or may be applied, are not subject to Sections 4 and 6 of Article VIII of the Ohio Constitution.

(F) The powers and authority granted or confirmed by and under this section, and the determinations and confirmations in this section, are independent of, in addition to, and not in derogation of or a limitation on, powers, authority, determinations, or confirmations under laws, charters, ordinances, or resolutions, or by or under other provisions of the Ohio Constitution including, without limitation, Section 36 of Article II, Sections 2i, 2l, 2m, 2o, and 13 of Article VIII, and Articles X and XVIII, and do not impair any previously adopted provision of the Ohio Constitution or any law previously enacted by the General Assembly.

(G) Obligations issued under this section, their transfer, and the interest, interest equivalent, and other income or accreted amounts on them, including any profit made on their sale, exchange, or other disposition, shall at all times be free from taxation within the state.

Section 2r. Issue bonds to provide compensation to veterans of the Persian Gulf, Afghanistan, and Iraq conflicts

(A) Upon the request of the department of veterans services, the Ohio public facilities commission shall proceed to issue and sell, from time to time, bonds or other obligations of the state in such amounts as are necessary to provide all or part of the funds as may be required to pay the compensation established by, and the expenses of administering, this section. The original principal amount of obligations so issued shall not exceed two hundred million dollars, provided that obligations issued under this section to retire or refund obligations previously issued under this section shall not be counted against that issuance limitation. The full faith and credit, revenue, and taxing power of the state is hereby pledged for payment of debt service on such obligations issued under this section, and the state covenants to continue the levy, collection, and application of sufficient state excises, taxes, and revenues to the extent needed for those purposes; provided that moneys referred to in Section 5a of Article XII of the Constitution of the State of Ohio may not be pledged or used for the payment of debt service. As used in this section, "debt service" means principal and interest and other accreted amounts payable on the obligations authorized by this section.

Each obligation so issued shall mature not later than the thirty-first day of December of the fifteenth calendar year after its issuance, except that obligations issued to refund obligations under this section shall mature not later than the thirty-first day of December of the fifteenth calendar year after the year in which the original obligation was issued. Except for obligations issued under this section to retire or refund obligations previously issued under this section, no obligations shall be issued under this section later than December 31, 2013.

In the case of the issuance of any obligations under this section as bond anticipation notes, provision shall be made in the bond or note proceedings for the establishment, and the maintenance during the period the notes are outstanding, of special funds into which there shall be paid, from the sources authorized for payment of the bonds anticipated, the amount that would have been sufficient to pay the principal that would have been payable on those bonds during that period if bonds maturing serially in each year over the maximum period of maturity referred to in this section had been issued without the prior issuance of the notes. Those special funds and investment income on them shall be used solely for the payment of debt service on those notes or the bonds anticipated.

The obligations issued under this section, their transfer, and the interest, interest equivalent, and other income thereon, including any profit made on their sale, exchange, or other disposition, shall at all times be free from taxation within the state.

Such obligations may be sold at public or private sale as determined by the Ohio public facilities commission.

(B) Out of the proceeds of the sale of all obligations, except those issued to refund or retire obligations previously issued under this section, the amount that represents accrued interest, if any, shall be paid into the state treasury into the Persian gulf, Afghanistan, and Iraq conflicts compensation bond retirement fund, which is hereby created. As determined at the time of sale, the amount that represents premium shall be paid into either the Persian gulf, Afghanistan, and Iraq conflicts compensation bond retirement fund or the Persian gulf, Afghanistan, and Iraq conflicts compensation fund, which is hereby created in the state treasury. The balance of the proceeds shall be paid into the Persian gulf, Afghanistan, and Iraq conflicts compensation fund. All proceeds of the sale of any obligations issued under this section to refund or retire obligations previously issued under this section shall be paid into the Persian gulf, Afghanistan, and Iraq conflicts compensation bond retirement fund and used to pay debt service on those outstanding obligations so refunded. The general assembly may appropriate and cause to be paid into the Persian gulf, Afghanistan, and Iraq conflicts compensation bond retirement fund or the Persian gulf, Afghanistan, and Iraq conflicts compensation fund, out of money in the treasury not otherwise appropriated, such amount as is proper for use for the purposes for which such funds are created. Except for amounts advanced by the general assembly to the Persian gulf, Afghanistan, and Iraq conflicts compensation fund with the express expectation of reimbursement from the proceeds of obligations paid into that fund, and except for amounts transferred under division (E) of this section for the purpose of defraying the immediate cost of administration and compensation, if the general assembly appropriates any funds to the Persian gulf, Afghanistan, and Iraq conflicts compensation fund prior to the time obligations have been issued in the original principal amount authorized in this section, that original principal amount authorized in this section shall be reduced by the amount of funds appropriated.

(C) On or before the fifteenth day of July of each fiscal year, the Ohio public facilities commission shall certify, or cause to be certified, to the director of budget and management the total amount of money required during the current fiscal year, together with all other money that will be available in the Persian gulf, Afghanistan, and Iraq conflicts compensation bond retirement fund, to meet in full all debt service and related financing costs on the obligations issued under this section. The director shall transfer from the general revenue fund to the Persian gulf, Afghanistan, and Iraq conflicts compensation bond retirement fund, without necessity of appropriation by the general assembly, an amount equal to the amount so certified, and those funds shall be used for the payment of the debt service.

(D)(1) The Persian gulf, Afghanistan, and Iraq conflicts compensation fund shall be paid out upon the order of the department of veterans services, without necessity of appropriation by the general assembly, in payment of the expenses of administering this section and as compensation as follows to each person who meets all of the following requirements:

(a) The person has served in active duty in the United States armed forces, except active duty for training only, at any time between August 2, 1990, and March 3, 1991, at any time between October 7, 2001, and the date determined by the president of the United States as the end of involvement of the United States armed forces in Afghanistan, or at any time between March 19, 2003, and the date determined by the president of the United States as the end of the involvement of the United States armed forces in Iraq.

(b) The person was an Ohio resident at the start of active duty service and is currently an Ohio resident.

(c) The person was separated from the United States armed forces under honorable conditions, is still serving in active duty service, or remains in any reserve component of the United States armed forces or in the Ohio national guard after serving on active duty.

A person who meets the requirements of divisions (D)(1)(a), (b), and (c) of this section is entitled to, and may apply to receive, compensation of fifty dollars for each month of active domestic or foreign service and one hundred dollars for each month of Persian gulf, Afghanistan, or Iraq service during the compensable periods. A person who is medically discharged or medically retired from service due to combat-related disabilities sustained during Persian gulf, Afghanistan, or Iraq service is entitled to, and may apply to receive, compensation of one thousand dollars. The maximum amount of cash payable to any person in active domestic or foreign service is five hundred dollars and the maximum amount of cash payable to any person in Persian gulf, Afghanistan, or Iraq service is one thousand dollars, unless the person qualifies for a survivor's payment or a payment based on missing in action or prisoner of war status under division (D)(2) or (D)(3) of this section. Compensation for a fraction of a month of service shall be paid on the basis of one-thirtieth of the appropriate monthly amount for each day of service.

(2) The surviving spouse, surviving child or children, or surviving parent or parents, including a person or persons standing in loco parentis for at least one year preceding commencement of service in the United States armed forces, is entitled to, and may apply to receive, the same amount of compensation that the person who served in the armed forces would have received under division (D)(1) of this section. If the United States department of veterans' affairs determines that the person's death was the result of injuries or illness sustained in Persian gulf, Afghanistan, or Iraq service, the person's survivors are entitled to, and may apply for, a survivor's payment of five thousand dollars, regardless of the amount of compensation that the deceased would have been entitled to receive under this section, if living. The survivor's payment shall be made to the surviving spouse. If there is no surviving spouse, the payment shall go to the surviving child or children. If there are no surviving children, the payment shall go to the surviving parent or parents or person or persons standing in loco parentis for at least one year preceding commencement of service in the United States armed forces.

(3) A person designated by the United States department of defense as missing in action as a result of honorable service or held in enemy captivity, or the spouse, child, or parent, including a person standing in loco parentis for at least one year preceding commencement of service in the United States armed forces, of a person designated as missing in action or held in enemy captivity, is entitled to, and may apply for, a payment of five thousand dollars. This payment replaces any other cash benefit payable under this section. While the person is missing or held captive, the payment shall be made to the person's spouse. If there is no spouse to claim the payment, payment shall be made to the person's child or children. If the person does not have children, payment shall be made to the person's parent or parents or person or persons standing in loco parentis for at least one year preceding commencement of service in the United States armed forces.

No payment to a spouse, child, parent, or person in loco parentis of a person designated as missing in action as a result of honorable service or held in enemy captivity, while the person is missing in action or held captive, shall prevent the missing or captive person from claiming and receiving a bonus of an equal amount on the person's release or location.

(4) Compensation shall not be paid under this section as follows:

(a) To any person who received from another state a bonus or compensation of a similar nature;

(b) To any person who served less than ninety days in the United States armed forces, unless active duty was terminated as a result of injuries or illness sustained during Persian gulf, Afghanistan, or Iraq service during the compensable period;

(c) To any person for any time period spent under penal confinement during the compensable period.

(5) No sale or assignment of any right or claim to compensation under this section shall be valid. No claims of creditors shall be enforceable against rights or claims to or payments of compensation under this section. No fees shall be charged for services in connection with the prosecution of any right or claim to compensation or the collection of any compensation under this section.

(6) All applications for payment of compensation under this section shall be made to the department of veterans services according to the following schedule:

(a) For Persian gulf service, not later than December 31, 2013;

(b) For Afghanistan service, not later than three years after the date determined by the president of the United States as the end of involvement of the United States armed forces in Afghanistan;

(c) For Iraq service, not later than three years after the date determined by the president of the United States as the end of involvement of the United States armed forces in Iraq.

(7) As used in this section:
"Afghanistan service" means military service within Afghanistan during the period between October 7, 2001, and the date determined by the president of the United States as the end of the involvement of the United States armed forces in Afghanistan.

"Domestic service" means service within the territorial limits of the fifty states.

"Foreign service" means service in locations other than the territorial limits of the fifty states, excluding Persian gulf, Afghanistan, or Iraq service.

"Iraq service" means military service within Iraq during the period between March 19, 2003, and the date determined by the president of the United States as the end of the involvement of the United States armed forces in Iraq.

"Persian gulf service" means military service within the Persian gulf theater of operations during the period between August 2, 1990, and March 3, 1991.

"United States armed forces" includes the army, air force, navy, marine corps, and coast guard; any active reserve component of such forces; and members of the Ohio national guard serving on active duty.

(E) The department of veterans services (hereinafter referred to as the "department") shall have complete charge of making payment of compensation under division (D) of this section and shall adopt rules, including rules regarding the amounts to which beneficiaries are entitled, residency requirements for purposes of division (D)(1)(b) of this section, and any other rules necessary to implement this section. These rules shall be adopted in accordance with Chapter 119. of the Revised Code.
The department shall select and appoint legal counsel and employees as are necessary and fix their compensation and prescribe their duties. All appointees shall serve at the pleasure of the director of veterans services. When practical, the department shall employ Persian gulf, Afghanistan, and Iraq conflict veterans to fill such positions. The general assembly shall transfer necessary funds to the Persian gulf, Afghanistan, and Iraq conflicts compensation fund and to the department's operating budget, for the purpose of defraying the immediate

cost of administration and compensation. Any funds so transferred shall not reduce the original principal amount of obligations that may be issued under this section.

On payment of all valid claims for cash compensation made within the time limitations under this section, the department may transfer any funds remaining in the Persian gulf, Afghanistan, and Iraq conflicts compensation fund to the Persian gulf, Afghanistan, and Iraq conflicts compensation bond retirement fund.

On retirement of all of the obligations issued under this section and payment of all valid claims for cash compensation made within the time limitations under this section, the department shall make a final report to the general assembly. Any balance remaining in the Persian gulf, Afghanistan, and Iraq conflicts compensation fund or the Persian gulf, Afghanistan, and Iraq conflicts compensation bond retirement fund shall be transferred or disposed of as provided by law.

Notwithstanding any other provision of this section to the contrary, valid claims for cash compensation made within the time limitations under this section shall be paid only if adequate funds remain in the Persian gulf, Afghanistan, and Iraq conflicts compensation fund.

(F) The people of this state declare it to be their intention that this amendment in no manner affects or changes any of the existing provisions of the Constitution except as set forth in this section. The provisions of this section shall be self-executing.

(G) Debt service on obligations issued pursuant to this section shall not be included in the calculation of total debt service for purposes of division (A) of Section 17 of Article VIII of the Constitution of the State of Ohio.

(H) As provided in divisions (C) and (D)(1) of this section, no further act of appropriation is necessary, notwithstanding Section 22 of Article II of the Constitution of the State of Ohio.

(I) Any reference in this section to a public office, officer, or body shall include any successor thereto.

Section 2s.

(A) In addition to the authorizations otherwise contained in Article VIII of the Ohio Constitution, the General Assembly may provide by law, in accordance with and subject to the limitations of this section, for the issuance of bonds and other obligations of the state for the purpose of financing or assisting in the financing of the cost of public infrastructure capital improvements of municipal corporations, counties, townships, and other governmental entities as designated by law. As used in this section, public infrastructure capital improvements shall be limited to roads and bridges, waste water treatment systems, water supply systems, solid waste disposal facilities, and storm water and sanitary collection, storage, and treatment facilities, including real property, interests in real property, facilities, and equipment related to or incidental thereto, and shall include, without limitation, the cost of acquisition, construction, reconstruction, expansion, improvement, planning, and equipping.

It is hereby determined that such public infrastructure capital improvements are necessary to preserve and expand the public capital infrastructure of such municipal corporations, counties, townships, and other governmental entities, ensure the public health, safety, and welfare, create and preserve jobs, enhance employment opportunities, and improve the economic welfare of the people of this state.

(B) Not more than one billion eight hundred seventy-five million dollars principal amount of state general obligations may be issued under this section for public infrastructure capital improvements. Not more than one hundred seventy-five million dollars principal amount of those obligations may be issued in each of the first five fiscal years of issuance and not more than two hundred million dollars principal amount of those obligations may be issued in each of the next five fiscal years of issuance, plus in each case the principal amount of those obligations that in any prior fiscal year could have been but were not issued within those fiscal year limits. No obligations may be issued pursuant to this section until all of the state infrastructure obligations authorized under Section 2p of Article VIII, Ohio Constitution have been issued.

(C) Each issue of obligations issued under this section shall mature in not more than thirty years from the date of issuance, or, if issued to retire or refund other obligations, within that number of years from the date the debt being retired or refunded was originally issued. If state general obligations are issued as notes in anticipation of the issuance of bonds, provision shall be made by law for the establishment and maintenance, during the period in which the notes are outstanding, of a special fund or funds into which shall be paid, from the sources authorized for the payment of such bonds, the amount that would have been sufficient, if bonds maturing during the permitted period of years had been issued without such prior issuance of notes, to pay the principal that would have been payable on such bonds during such period. Such fund or funds shall be used solely for the payment of principal of such notes or bonds in anticipation of which such notes have been issued. Obligations issued under this section to retire or refund obligations previously issued under this section or Section 2k, 2m, or 2p shall not be counted against the fiscal year or total issuance limitations provided in this section or Section 2k, 2m, or 2p, as applicable.

(D) The obligations issued under this section are general obligations of the state. The full faith and credit, revenue, and taxing power of the state shall be pledged to the payment of the principal of and premium and interest and other accreted amounts on outstanding obligations as they become due (hereinafter called debt service), and bond retirement fund provisions shall be made for payment of that debt service. Provision shall be made by law for the sufficiency and appropriation, for purposes of paying debt service, of excises, taxes, and revenues so pledged or committed to debt service, and for covenants to continue the levy, collection, and application of sufficient excises, taxes, and revenues to the extent needed for that purpose. Notwithstanding Section 22 of Article II, Ohio Constitution, no further act of appropriation shall be necessary for that purpose. The obligations and the provision for the payment of debt service, and repayment by governmental entities of any loans made under this section, are not subject to Sections 5, 6, and 11 of Article XII, Ohio Constitution. Moneys referred to in Section 5a of Article XII, Ohio Constitution may not be pledged to the payment of that debt service.

(E) The state may participate in any public infrastructure capital improvement under this section with municipal corporations, counties, townships, or other governmental entities as designated by law, or any one or more of them. Such participation may be by grants, loans, or contributions to them for any such capital improvements. The entire proceeds of the infrastructure obligations shall be used for public infrastructure capital improvements of municipal corporations, counties, townships, and other governmental entities, except to the extent that the General Assembly provides by law that the state may reasonably be compensated from such moneys for planning, financial management, or administrative services performed in relation to the issuance of infrastructure obligations.

(F) Obligations issued under authority of this section, the transfer thereof, and the interest, interest equivalent, and other income and accreted amounts therefrom, including any profit made on the sale, exchange, or other disposition thereof, shall at all times be free from taxation within the state.

(G) This section shall otherwise be implemented in the manner and to the extent provided by law by the General Assembly, including provision for the procedure for incurring and issuing obligations, separately or in combination with other obligations, and refunding, retiring, and evidencing obligations, and provision for the use to the extent practicable of Ohio products, materials, services, and labor in the making of any project financed, in whole or in part, under this section.

(H) The powers and authority granted or confirmed by and under, and the determinations in, this section are independent of, in addition to, and not in derogation of or a limitation on, powers, authority, determinations, or confirmations under laws or under other provisions of the Ohio Constitution and do not impair any previously adopted provisions of the Ohio Constitution or any law previously enacted by the General Assembly or by a local public agency.

Section 3. The State to Create No Other Debt; Exceptions

Except the debts above specified in sections one and two of this article, no debt whatever shall hereafter be created by or on behalf of the state.

Section 4. Credit of State; the State Shall Not Become Joint Owner or Stockholder

The credit of the state shall not, in any manner, be given or loaned to, or in aid of, any individual association or corporation whatever; nor shall the state ever hereafter become a joint owner, or stockholder, in any company or association in this state, or elsewhere, formed for any purpose whatever.

Section 5. No Assumption of Debts by the State

The state shall never assume the debts of any county, city, town, or township, or of any corporation whatever, unless such debt shall have been created to repel invasion, suppress insurrection, or defend the state in war.

Section 6. Countries, Cities, Towns, or Townships, Not Authorized to Become Stockholders, Etc.; Insurance, Etc.

No laws shall be passed authorizing any county, city, town or township, by vote of its citizens, or otherwise, to become a stockholder in any joint stock company, corporation, or association whatever; or to raise money for, or to loan its credit to, or in aid of, any such company, corporation, or association: provided, that nothing in this section shall prevent the insuring of public buildings or property in mutual insurance associations or companies. Laws may be passed providing for the regulation of all rates charged or to be charged by any insurance company, corporation or association organized under the laws of this state, or doing any insurance business in this state for profit.

Section 7. Sinking Fund

The faith of the state being pledged for the payment of its public debt, in order to provide therefore, there shall be created a sinking fund, which shall be sufficient to pay the accruing interest on such debt, and, annually, to reduce the principal thereof, by a sum not less than one hundred thousand dollars, increased yearly, and each and every year, by compounding, at the rate of six per cent per annum. The said sinking fund shall consist, of the net annual income of the public works and stocks owned by the state, of any other funds or resources that are, or may be, provided by law, and of such further sum, to be raised by taxation, as may be required for the purposes aforesaid.

Section 8. The Commissioners of the Sinking Fund
The governor, treasurer of state, auditor of state, secretary of state, and attorney general, are hereby created a board of commissioners, to be styled, "The Commissioners of the Sinking Fund."

Section 9. Biennial Report of Sinking Fund Commissioners

The commissioners of the sinking fund shall, immediately preceding each regular session of the General Assembly, make an estimate of the probable amount of the fund, provided for in the seventh section of this article, from all sources except from taxation, and report the same, together with all their proceedings relative to said fund and the public debt, to the governor, who shall transmit the same with his regular message, to the General Assembly; and the General Assembly shall make all necessary provision for raising and disbursing said sinking fund, in pursuance of the provisions of this article.

Section 10. Application of Sinking Fund

It shall be the duty of the said commissioners faithfully to apply said fund, together with all moneys that may be, by the General Assembly, appropriated to that object, to the payment of the interest, as it becomes due, and the redemption of the principal of the public debt of the state, excepting only, the school and trust funds held by the state.

Section 11. Semiannual Report of Sinking Fund Commissioners
The said commissioners shall, semiannually, make a full and detailed report of their proceedings to the governor, who shall, immediately, cause the same to be published, and shall also communicate the same to the General Assembly, forthwith, if it be in session, and if not, then at its first session after such report shall be made.

Section 12. Repealed

Section 13. Economic Development

To create or preserve jobs and employment opportunities, to improve the economic welfare of the people of the state, to control air, water, and thermal pollution, or to dispose of solid waste, it is hereby determined to be in the public interest and a proper public purpose for the state or its political subdivisions, taxing districts, or public authorities, its or their agencies or instrumentalities, or corporations not for profit designated by any of them as such agencies or instrumentalities, to acquire, construct, enlarge, improve, or equip, and to sell, lease, exchange, or otherwise dispose of property, structures, equipment, and facilities within the state of Ohio for industry, commerce, distribution, and research, to make or guarantee loans and to borrow money and issue bonds or other obligations to provide moneys for the acquisition, construction, enlargement, improvement, or equipment, of such property, structures, equipment and facilities. Laws may be passed to carry into effect such purposes and to authorize for such purposes the borrowing of money by, and the issuance of bonds or other obligations of, the state, or its political subdivisions, taxing districts, or public authorities, its or their agencies or instrumentalities, or corporations not for profit designated by any of them as such agencies or instrumentalities, and to authorize the guarantees and loans and the lending of aid and credit, which laws, bonds, obligations, loans and guarantees, and lending of aid and credit shall not be subject to the requirements, limitations or prohibitions of any other section of Article VIII, or of Article XII, Sections 6 and 11, of the Constitution, provided that moneys raised by taxation shall not be obligated or pledged for the payment of bonds or other obligations issued or guarantees made pursuant to laws enacted under this section. Except for facilities for pollution control or solid waste disposal, as determined by law, no guarantees or loans and no lending of aid or credit shall be made under the laws enacted pursuant to this section of the constitution for facilities to be constructed for the purpose of providing electric or gas utility service to the public. The powers herein granted shall be in addition to and not in derogation of existing powers of the state or its political subdivisions, taxing districts, or public authorities, or their agencies or instrumentalities or corporations not for profit designated by any of them as such agencies or instrumentalities. Any corporation organized under the laws of Ohio is hereby authorized to lend or contribute moneys to the state or its political subdivisions or agencies or instrumentalities thereof on such terms as may be agreed upon in furtherance of laws enacted pursuant to this section.

Section 14. Financing for Housing Program

To create or preserve opportunities for safe and sanitary housing and to improve the economic welfare of the people of the state, it is hereby determined to be in the public interest and a proper public purpose for the state to borrow money and issue bonds and other obligations to make available financing, at reasonable interest rates to consumers substantially reflecting savings in the cost of money to lenders resulting from the implementation of this section, for the acquisition, construction, rehabilitation, remodeling, and improvement of privately owned multiple-unit dwellings used and occupied exclusively by persons sixty-two years of age and older, and privately owned, owner occupied single family housing by providing loans to, or through the agency of, or originated by, or purchasing loans from, persons regularly engaged in the business of making or brokering residential mortgage loans, all as determined by or pursuant to law. Laws may be passed to carry into effect such purpose and to authorize for such purpose the borrowing of money by, and the issuance of bonds or other obligations of the state and to authorize the making of such loans, which laws, bonds, obligations, and loans shall not be subject to the requirements, limitations, or prohibitions of any other section of Article VIII, or Sections 6 and 11 of Article XII, Ohio Constitution, provided that moneys raised by taxation shall not be obligated or pledged for the payment of bonds or other obligations issued pursuant to laws enacted under this section. The powers granted in this section shall be in addition to and not in derogation of existing powers of the state. Any corporation organized under the laws of this state may lend or contribute moneys to the state on such terms as may be agreed upon in furtherance of laws enacted pursuant to this section.

Section 15. State Assistance to Development of Coal Technology

Laws may be passed authorizing the state to borrow money and to issue bonds and other obligations for the purpose of making grants and making or guaranteeing loans for research and development of coal technology that will encourage the use of Ohio coal, to any individual, association, or corporation doing business in this state, or to any educational or scientific institution located in this state, notwithstanding the requirements, limitation, or prohibitions of any other section of Article VIII or of section 6 and 11 of Article XII of the constitution. The aggregate principal amount of the money borrowed and bonds and other obligations issued by the state pursuant to laws passed under this section shall not exceed one hundred million dollars outstanding at any time. The full faith and credit of the state may be pledged for the payment of bonds or other obligations issued or guarantees made pursuant to laws passed under this section Laws passed pursuant to this section also may provide for the state to share in any royalties, profits, or other financial gain resulting from the research and development.

Section 16. State and Political Subdivisions to Provide Housing for Individuals

To enhance the availability of adequate housing in the state and to improve the economic and general well-being of the people of the state, it is determined to be in the public interest and a proper public purpose for the state or its political subdivisions, directly or through a public authority, agency, or instrumentality, to provide, or assist in providing, by grants, loans, subsidies to loans, loans to lenders, purchases of loans, guarantees of loans, or otherwise as determined by the General Assembly, housing, including shelters to provide temporary housing in the state for individuals and families by the acquisition, financing, construction, leasing, rehabilitation, remodeling, improvement, or equipping of publicly or privately owned housing, including the acquisition of real property and interests in real property. Laws, including charters, ordinances, and resolutions, may be passed to carry into effect those purposes, including but not limited to the authorization of the making of grants, loans, subsidies to loans, loans to lenders, purchase of loans, and guarantees of loans by the state or its political subdivisions, directly or through a public authority, agency, or instrumentality, which laws, charters, ordinances, resolutions, grants, loans subsidies to loans, loans to lenders, purchase of loans, guarantees of loans, and any other actions authorized by the General Assembly shall not be subject to the requirements, limitations, or prohibitions of any other section of Article VIII, or sections 6 and 11 of Article XII, Ohio Constitution. The General Assembly also may authorize the issuance by the state, directly or through its public authorities, agencies, or instrumentalities, of obligations to provide moneys for the provision of or assistance in the provision of housing, including shelters to provide temporary housing, in the state for individuals and families, which obligations are not supported by the full faith and credit of the state, and shall not be deemed to be debts or bonded indebtedness of the state under other provisions of this Constitution. Such obligations may be secured by a pledge under law, without necessity for further appropriation, of all or such portion as the General Assembly authorizes of revenues or receipts of the state or its public authorities, agencies, or instrumentalities, and this provision may be implemented by law to better provide therefore. The powers granted under this section are independent of, in addition to, and not in derogation of other powers under laws, charters, ordinances, resolutions, or this Constitution including the powers granted under section 14 of Article VIII and Articles X and XVIII, and the provision of any capital improvements under section 2i of

Article VIII, Ohio Constitution. The powers granted under this section do not impair any law, charter, ordinance, or resolution enacted prior to the effective date of this section or any obligations issued under such law charter, ordinance, or resolution. The powers granted under this section are subject to the power of the General Assembly to regulate taxation and debt of political subdivisions, including the regulation of municipal taxation and debt pursuant to section 6 of Article XIII and section 13 Article XVIII, Ohio Constitution. The powers granted to political subdivisions under this section shall be operative on and after September 1, 1991, or on an earlier date that an act of the General Assembly declares such powers shall be operative.

Section 17. Limitations on Obligations State May Issue

(A) Direct obligations of the state may not be issued under this article if the amount required to be applied or set aside in any future fiscal year for payment of debt service on direct obligations of the state to be outstanding in accordance with their terms during such future fiscal year would exceed five per cent of the total estimated revenues of the state for the General Revenue Fund and from net state lottery proceeds during the fiscal year in which the particular obligations are to be issued. As used in this division, "debt service" includes the debt service on the bonds to be issued under this article that are direct obligations of the state plus, if the obligations to be issued are bond anticipation notes, the debt service on the bonds anticipated, plus the debt service on all other outstanding bonds that are direct obligations of the state, to the extent that debt service on all those bonds and bonds anticipated is to be paid from the General Revenue Fund or net state lottery proceeds.

(B) The limitations of division (A) of this section shall not apply to a particular issue or amount of obligations if the limitations are waived as to that particular issue or amount by the affirmative vote of at least three-fifths of the members of each house of the General Assembly, or to obligations issued to retire bond anticipation notes that were issued when the requirements of division (A) of this section were originally met as estimated for the bonds anticipated.

(C) For purposes of division (A) of this section, debt contracted by the state pursuant to Section 2 of Article VIII of the Ohio Constitution to repel invasion, suppress insurrection, or to defend the state in war, shall not be included in the calculation of total debt service.

(D) For purposes of division (A) of this section, the General Assembly shall provide by law for computing the amounts required for payment of debt service, and may provide for estimating payments of debt service on bonds anticipated by notes, for including payments of debt service on obligations issued to refund or retire prior obligations in lieu of such payments on the prior refunded or retired obligations, and for the method of computing payments of debt service on any obligations required to be retired or for which sinking fund deposits are required prior to stated maturity. The Governor or the Governor's designee for such purpose shall determine and certify the fiscal year amounts required to be applied or set aside for payment of debt service, the obligations to which that debt service relates, the total estimated revenues of the state for the state General Revenue Fund and from net state lottery proceeds during the particular fiscal year, other financial data necessary for the purposes of computations under division (A) of this section, and the permitted latest maturity of obligations. That certification shall be conclusive for the purposes of the validity of any obligations issued under this article.

(E) As used in this section:

(1) "Fiscal year" means the state fiscal year.

(2) "Debt service" means principal and interest and other accreted amounts payable on the obligations referred to.

(3) "Direct obligations of the state" means obligations issued by the state on which the state of Ohio is the primary or only direct obligor.

ARTICLE IX: MILITIA

Section 1. Who Shall Perform Military Duty

All citizens, residents of this state, being seventeen years of age, and under the age of sixty-seven years, shall be subject to enrollment in the militia and the performance of military duty, in such manner, not incompatible with the Constitution and laws of the United States, as may be prescribed by law.

Section 2. Repealed

Section 3. Appointment of Militia Officers

The governor shall appoint the adjutant general, and such other officers and warrant officers, as may be provided for by law.

Section 4. Power of Governor to Call Forth Militia

The governor shall have power to call forth the militia, to execute the laws of the state, to suppress insurrection, to repel invasion, and to act in the event of a disaster within the state.

Section 5. Public Arms; Arsenals

The General Assembly shall provide, by law, for the protection and safe keeping of the public arms.

ARTICLE X: COUNTY AND TOWNSHIP ORGANIZATIONS

Section 1. Organization and Government of Counties; County Home Rule; Submission

The General Assembly shall provide by general law for the organization and government of counties, and may provide by general law alternative forms of county government. No alternative form shall become operative in any county until submitted to the electors thereof and approved by a majority of those voting thereon under regulations provided by law. Municipalities and townships shall have authority, with the consent of the county, to transfer to the county any of their powers or to revoke the transfer of any such power, under regulations provided by general law, but the rights of initiative and referendum shall be secured to the people of such municipalities or townships in respect of every measure making or revoking such transfer and to the people of such county in respect of every measure giving or withdrawing such consent.

Section 2. Township Officers; Election; Power

The General Assembly shall provide by general law for the election of such township officers as may be necessary. The trustees of townships shall have such powers of local taxation as may be prescribed by law. No money shall be drawn from any township treasury except by authority of law.

Section 3. County Charters; Approval by Voters

The people of any county may frame and adopt or amend a charter as provided in this article but the right of the initiative and referendum is reserved to the people of each county on all matters which such county may now or hereafter be authorized to control by legislative action. Every such charter shall provide the form of government of the county and shall determine which of its officers shall be elected and the manner of their election. It shall provide for the exercise of all powers vested in, and the performance of all duties imposed upon counties and county officers by law. Any such charter may provide for the concurrent or exclusive exercise by the county, in all or in part of its area, of all or of any designated powers vested by the constitution or laws of Ohio in municipalities; it may provide for the organization of the county as a municipal corporation; and in any such case it may provide for the succession by the county to the rights, properties, and obligations of municipalities and townships therein incident to the municipal power so vested in the county, and for the division of the county into districts for purposes of administration or of taxation or of both. Any charter or amendment which alters the form and offices of county government or which provides for the exercise by the county of power vested in municipalities by the constitution or laws of Ohio, or both, shall become effective if approved by a majority of the electors voting thereon. In case of conflict between the exercise of powers granted by such charter and the exercise of powers by municipalities or townships, granted by the constitution or general law, whether or not such powers are being exercised at the time of the adoption of the charter, the exercise of power by the municipality or township shall prevail. A charter or amendment providing for the exclusive exercise of municipal powers by the county or providing for the succession by the county to any property or obligation of any municipality or township without the consent of the legislative authority of such municipality or township shall become effective only when it shall have been approved by a majority of those voting thereon (1) in the county, (2) in the largest municipality, (3) in the county outside of such municipality, and (4) in counties having a population, based upon the latest preceding federal decennial census of 500,000 or less, in each of a majority of the combined total of municipalities and townships in the county (not included within any township any part of its area lying within a municipality.

Section 4. County Charter Commission; Election, Etc.

The legislative authority (which includes the Board of County Commissioners) of any county may by a two-thirds vote of its members, or upon petition of eight per cent of the electors of the county as certified by the election authorities of the county shall forthwith, by resolution submit to the electors of the county the question, 'Shall a county charter commission be chosen?" The question shall be voted upon at the next general election, occurring not sooner than ninety-five days after certification of the resolution to the election authorities. The ballot containing the question shall bear no party designation. Provision shall be made thereon for the election to such commission from the county at large of fifteen electors if a majority of the electors voting on the question have voted in the affirmative. Candidates for such commission shall be nominated by petition of one per cent of the electors of the county. The petition shall be filed with the election authorities no less than seventy-five days prior to such election. Candidates shall be declared elected in the order of the number of votes received, beginning with the candidate receiving the largest number; but not more than seven candidates residing in the same city or village may be elected. The holding of a public office does not preclude any person from seeking or holding membership on a county charter commission nor does membership on a county charter commission preclude any such member from seeking or holding other public office, but not more than four officeholders may be elected to a county charter commission at the same time. The legislative authority shall appropriate sufficient sums to enable the charter commission to perform its duties and to pay all reasonable expenses thereof. The commission shall frame a charter for the county or amendments to the existing charter, and shall, by vote of a majority of the authorized number of members of the commission, submit the same to the electors of the county, to be voted upon at the next general election next following the election of the commission. The commission shall certify the proposed charter or amendments to the election authorities not later than seventy-five days prior to such election. Amendments to a county charter or the question of the repeal thereof may also be submitted to the electors of the county in the manner provided in this section for the submission of the question whether a charter commission shall be chosen, to be voted upon at the first general election occurring not sooner than sixty days after their submission. The legislative authority or charter commission submitting any charter or amendment shall, not later than thirty days prior to the election on such charter or amendment, mail or otherwise distribute a copy thereof to each of the electors of the county as far as may be reasonably possible, except that, as provided by law, notice of proposed amendments may be given by newspaper advertising. Except as provided in Section 3 of this Article, every charter or amendment shall become effective if it has been approved by the majority of the electors voting thereon. It shall take effect on the thirtieth day after such approval unless another date be fixed therein. When more than one amendment, which shall relate to only one subject but may affect or include more than one section or part of a charter, is submitted at the same time, they shall be so submitted as to enable the electors to vote on each separately. In case more than one charter is submitted at the same time or in case of conflict between the provisions of two or more amendments submitted at the same time, that charter or provision shall prevail which received the highest affirmative vote, not less than a majority. If a charter or amendment submitted by a charter commission is not approved by the electors of the county, the charter commission may resubmit the same one time, in its original form or as revised by the charter commission, to the electors of the county at the next succeeding general election or at any other election held throughout the county prior thereto, in the manner provided for the original submission thereof. The legislative authority of any county, upon petition of ten per cent of the electors of the county, shall forthwith, by resolution, submit to the electors of the county, in the manner provided in this section for the submission of the question whether a charter commission shall be chosen, the question of the adoption of a charter in the form attached to such petition. Laws may be passed to provide for the organization and procedures of county charter commissions, including the filling of any vacancy which may occur, and otherwise to facilitate the operation of this section. The basis upon which the required number of petitioners in any case provided for in this section shall be determined, shall be the total number of votes cast in the county for the office of governor at the last preceding general election therefore. The foregoing provisions of this section shall be self-executing except as herein otherwise provided.

Section 5. Repealed

Section 6. Repealed

Section 7. Repealed

ARTICLE XI: APPORTIONMENT

Section 1.

(A) The Ohio redistricting commission shall be responsible for the redistricting of this state for the general assembly. The commission shall consist of the following seven members:

(1) The governor;

(2) The auditor of state;

(3) The secretary of state;

(4) One person appointed by the speaker of the house of representatives;

(5) One person appointed by the legislative leader of the largest political party in the house of representatives of which the speaker of the house of representatives is not a member;

(6) One person appointed by the president of the senate; and

(7) One person appointed by the legislative leader of the largest political party in the senate of which the president of the senate is not a member.

No appointed member of the commission shall be a current member of congress.

The legislative leaders in the senate and the house of representatives of each of the two largest political parties represented in the general assembly, acting jointly by political party. shall appoint a member of the commission to serve as a co-chairperson of the commission.

(B)(1) Unless otherwise specified in this article or in Article XIX of this constitution, a simple majority of the commission members shall be required for any action by the commission.

(2)(a) Except as otherwise provided in division (B)(2)(b) of this section, a majority vote of the members of the commission including at least one member of the commission who is a member of each of the two largest political parties represented in the general assembly, shall be required to do any of the following:

(i) Adopt rules of the commission;

(ii) Hire staff for the commission;

(iii) Expend funds.

(b) If the commission is unable to agree, by the vote required under division (B)(2)(a) of this section. on the manner in which funds should be expended, each co-chairperson of the commission shall have the authority to expend one-half of the funds that have been appropriated to the commission.

(3) The affirmative vote of four members of the commission, including at least two members of the commission who represent each of the two largest political parties represented in the general assembly shall be required to adopt any general assembly district plan. For the purposes of this division and of Section 1 of Article XIX of this constitution, a member of the commission shall be considered to represent a political party if the member was appointed to the commission by a member of that political party or if, in the case of the governor, the auditor of state, or the secretary of state, the member is a member of that political party.

(C) At the first meeting of the commission, which the governor shall convene only in a year ending in the numeral one, except as provided in Sections 8 and 9 of this article and in Sections 1 and 3 of Article XIX of this constitution, the commission shall set a schedule for the adoption of procedural rules for the operation of the commission.

The commission shall release to the public a proposed general assembly district plan for the boundaries for each of the ninety-nine house of representatives districts and the thirty-three senate districts. The commission shall draft the proposed plan in the manner prescribed in this article. Before adopting, but after introducing, a proposed plan, the commission shall conduct a minimum of three public hearings across the state to present the proposed plan and shall seek public input regarding the proposed plan. All meetings of the commission shall be open to the public. Meetings shall be broadcast by electronic means of transmission using a medium readily accessible by the general public.
The commission shall adopt a final general assembly district plan not later than the first day of September of a year ending in the numeral one. After the commission adopts a final plan, the commission shall promptly file the plan with the secretary of state. Upon filing with the secretary of state, the plan shall become effective.

Four weeks after the adoption of a general assembly district plan or a congressional district plan, whichever is later, the commission shall be automatically dissolved.

(D) The general assembly shall be responsible for making the appropriations it determines necessary in order for the commission to perform its duties under this article and Article XIX of this constitution.

Section 2. Each house of representatives district shall be entitled to a single representative in each general assembly. Each senate district shall be entitled to a single senator in each general assembly.

Section 3.

(A) The whole population of the state, as determined by the federal decennial census or, if such is unavailable, such other basis as the general assembly may direct, shall be divided by the number "ninety-nine" and by the number "thirty-three" and the quotients shall be the ratio of representation in the house of representatives and in the senate, respectively, for ten years next succeeding such redistricting.

(B) A general assembly district plan shall comply with all of the requirements of division (B) of this section.

(1) The population of each house of representatives district shall be substantially equal to the ratio of representation in the house of representatives, and the population of each senate district shall be substantially equal to the ratio of representation in the senate, as provided in division (A) of this section. In no event shall any district contain a population of less than ninety-five per cent nor more than one hundred five per cent of the applicable ratio of representation.

(2) Any general assembly district plan adopted by the commission shall comply with all applicable provisions of the constitutions of Ohio and the United States and of federal law.

(3) Every general assembly district shall be composed of contiguous territory, and the boundary of each district shall be a single non-intersecting continuous line.

(C) House of representatives districts shall be created and numbered in the following order of priority. to the extent that such order is consistent with the foregoing standards:

(1) Proceeding in succession from the largest to the smallest, each county containing population greater than one hundred five per cent of the ratio of representation in the house of representatives shall be divided into as many house of representatives districts as it has whole ratios of representation. Any fraction of the population in excess of a whole ratio shall be a part of only one adjoining house of representatives district.

(2) Each county containing population of not less than ninety-five per cent of the ratio of representation in the house of representatives nor more than one hundred five per cent of the ratio shall be designated a representative district.

(3) The remaining territory of the state shall be divided into representative districts by combining the areas of counties, municipal corporations, and townships. Where feasible, no county shall be split more than once.

(D)(1)(a) Except as otherwise provided in divisions (D)(l)(b) and (c) of this section, a county, municipal corporation, or township is considered to be split if any contiguous portion of its territory is not contained entirely within one district.

(b) If a municipal corporation or township has territory in more than one county, the contiguous portion of that municipal corporation or township that lies in each county shall be considered to be a separate municipal corporation or township for the purposes of this section.

(c) If a municipal corporation or township that is located in a county that contains a municipal corporation or township that has a population of more than one ratio of representation is split for the purpose of complying with division (E)(l)(a) or (b) of this section, each portion of that municipal corporation or township shall be considered to be a separate municipal corporation or township for the purposes of this section.

(2) Representative districts shall be drawn so as to split the smallest possible number of municipal corporations and townships whose contiguous portions contain a population of more than fifty per cent. but less than one hundred per cent, of one ratio of representation.

(3) Where the requirements of divisions (B), (C), and (D) of this section cannot feasibly be attained by forming a representative district from whole municipal corporations and townships, not more than one municipal corporation or township may be split per representative district.

(E)(1) If it is not possible for the commission to comply with all of the requirements of divisions (B), (C), and (D) of this section in drawing a particular representative district, the commission shall take the first action listed below that makes it possible for the commission to draw that district:

(a) Notwithstanding division (D)(3) of this section, the commission shall create the district by splitting two municipal corporations or townships whose contiguous portions do not contain a population of more than fifty per cent, but less than one hundred per cent, of one ratio of representation.

(b) Notwithstanding division (D)(2) of this section, the commission shall create the district by splitting a municipal corporation or township whose contiguous portions contain a population of more than fifty per cent, but less than one hundred per cent, of one ratio of representation.

(c) Notwithstanding division (C)(2) of this section, the commission shall create the district by splitting, once, a single county that contains a population of not less than ninety-five per cent of the ratio of representation, but not more than one hundred five per cent of the ratio of representation.

(d) Notwithstanding division (C)(l) of this section, the commission shall create the district by including in two districts portions of the territory that remains after a county that contains a population of more than one hundred five per cent of the ratio of representation has been divided into as many house of representatives districts as it has whole ratios of representation.

(2) If the commission takes an action under division (E)(1) of this section, the commission shall include in the general assembly district plan a statement explaining which action the commission took under that division and the reason the commission took that action.

(3) If the commission complies with divisions (E)(1) and (2) of this section in drawing a district, the commission shall not be considered to have violated division (C)(l), (C)(2), (D)(2), or (D)(3) of this section, as applicable, in drawing that district. for the purpose of an analysis under division (D) of Section 9 of this article.

Section 4.

(A) Senate districts shall be composed of three contiguous house of representatives districts.

(B)(1) A county having at least one whole senate ratio of representation shall have as many senate districts wholly within the boundaries of the county as it has whole senate ratios of representation. Any fraction of the population in excess of a whole ratio shall be a part of only one adjoining senate district.

(2) Counties having less than one senate ratio of representation, but at least one house of representatives ratio of representation, shall be part of only one senate district.

(3) If it is not possible for the commission to draw representative districts that comply with all of the requirements of this article and that make it possible for the commission to comply with all of the requirements of divisions (B)(1) and (2) of this section, the commission shall draw senate districts so as to commit the fewest possible violations of those divisions. If the commission complies with this division in drawing senate districts, the commission shall not be considered to have violated division (B)(1) or (2) of this section, as applicable, in drawing those districts, for the purpose of an analysis under division (D) of Section 9 of this article.

(C) The number of whole ratios of representation for a county shall be determined by dividing the population of the county by the ratio of representation in the senate determined under division (A) of Section 3 of this article.

(D) Senate districts shall be numbered from one through thirty-three and as provided in Section 5 of this article.

Section 5. At any time the boundaries of senate districts are changed in any general assembly district plan made pursuant to any provision of this article, a senator whose term will not expire within two years of the time the plan becomes effective shall represent, for the remainder of the term for which the senator was elected. the senate district that contains the largest portion of the population of the district from which the senator was elected, and the district shall be given the number of the district from which the senator was elected. If more than one senator whose term will not so expire would represent the same district by following the provisions of this section, the plan shall designate which senator shall represent the district and shall designate which district the other senator or senators shall represent for the balance of their term or terms.

Section 6. The Ohio redistricting commission shall attempt to draw a general assembly district plan that meets all of the following standards:

(A) No general assembly district plan shall be drawn primarily to favor or disfavor a political party.

(B) The statewide proportion of districts whose voters, based on statewide state and federal partisan general election results during the last ten years, favor each political party shall correspond closely to the statewide preferences of the voters of Ohio.

(C) General assembly districts shall be compact. Nothing in this section permits the commission to violate the district standards described in Section 2, 3, 4, 5, or 7 of this article.

Section 7. Notwithstanding the fact that boundaries of counties, municipal corporations, and townships within a district may be changed, district boundaries shall be created by using the boundaries of counties, municipal corporations. and townships as they exist at the time of the federal decennial census on which the redistricting is based, or, if unavailable, on such other basis as the general assembly has directed.

Section 8.

(A)(1) If the Ohio redistricting commission fails to adopt a final general assembly district plan not later than the first day of September of a year ending in the numeral one. in accordance with Section 1 of this article, the commission shall introduce a proposed general assembly district plan by a simple majority vote of the commission.

(2) After introducing a proposed general assembly district plan under division (A)(1) of this section, the commission shall hold a public hearing concerning the proposed plan, at which the public may offer testimony and at which the commission may adopt amendments to the proposed plan. Members of the commission should attend the hearing; however, only a quorum of the members of the commission is required to conduct the hearing.

(3) After the hearing described in division (A)(2) of this section is held, and not later than the fifteenth day of September of a year ending in the numeral one, the commission shall adopt a final general assembly district plan, either by the vote required to adopt a plan under division (B)(3) of Section 1 of this article or by a simple majority vote of the commission.

(B) If the commission adopts a final general assembly district plan in accordance with division (A)(3) of this section by the vote required to adopt a plan under division (B)(3) of Section 1 of this article, the plan shall take effect upon filing with the secretary of state and shall remain effective until the next year ending in the numeral one, except as provided in Section 9 of this article.

(C)(1)(a) Except as otherwise provided in division (C)(1)(b) of this section, if the commission adopts a final general assembly district plan in accordance with division (A)(3) of this section by a simple majority vote of the commission, and not by the vote required to adopt a plan under division (B)(3) of Section 1 of this article, the plan shall take effect upon filing with the secretary of state and shall remain effective until two general elections for the house of representatives have occurred under the plan.

(b) If the commission adopts a final general assembly district plan in accordance with division (A)(3) of this section by a simple majority vote of the commission, and not by the vote required to adopt a plan under division (B) of Section 1 of this article, and that plan is adopted to replace a plan that ceased to be effective under division (C)(l)(a) of this section before a year ending in the numeral one, the plan adopted under this division shall take effect upon filing with the secretary of state and shall remain effective until a year ending in the numeral one, except as provided in Section 9 of this article.

(2) A final general assembly district plan adopted under division (C)(1)(a) or (b) of this section shall include a statement explaining what the commission determined to be the statewide preferences of the voters of Ohio and the manner in which the statewide proportion of districts in the plan whose voters, based on statewide state and federal partisan general election results during the last ten years, favor each political party corresponds closely to those preferences, as described in division (B) of Section 6 of this article. At the time the plan is adopted, a member of the commission who does not vote in favor of the plan may submit a declaration of the member's opinion concerning the statement included with the plan.

(D) After a general assembly district plan adopted under division (C)(1)(a) of this section ceases to be effective, and not earlier than the first day of July of the year following the year in which the plan ceased to be effective, the commission shall be reconstituted as provided in Section 1 of this article, convene. and adopt a new general assembly district plan in accordance with this article, to be used until the next time for redistricting under this article. The commission shall draw the new general assembly district plan using the same population and county, municipal corporation, and township boundary data as were used to draw the previous plan adopted under division (C) of this section.

Section 9.

(A) The supreme court of Ohio shall have exclusive, original jurisdiction in all cases arising under this article.

(B) In the event that any section of this constitution relating to redistricting, any general assembly district plan made by the Ohio redistricting commission, or any district is determined to be invalid by an un-appealed final order of a court of competent jurisdiction then, notwithstanding any other provisions of this constitution, the commission shall be reconstituted as provided in Section 1 of this article, convene, and ascertain and determine a general assembly district plan in conformity with such provisions of this constitution as are then valid, including establishing terms of office and election of members of the general assembly from districts designated in the plan, to be used until the next time for redistricting under this article in conformity with such provisions of this constitution as are then valid.

(C) Notwithstanding any provision of this constitution or any law regarding the residence of senators and representatives, a general assembly district plan made pursuant to this section shall allow thirty days for persons to change residence in order to be eligible for election.

(D)(1) No court shall order, in any circumstance, the implementation or enforcement of any general assembly district plan that has not been approved by the commission in the manner prescribed by this article.

(2) No court shall order the commission to adopt a particular general assembly district plan or to draw a particular district.

(3) If the supreme court of Ohio determines that a general assembly district plan adopted by the commission does not comply with the requirements of Section 2, 3, 4, 5, or 7 of this article, the available remedies shall be as follows:

(a) If the court finds that the plan contains one or more isolated violations of those requirements. the court shall order the commission to amend the plan to correct the violation.

(b) If the court finds that it is necessary to amend not fewer than six house of representatives districts to correct violations of those requirements, to amend not fewer than two senate districts to correct violations of those requirements. or both, the court shall declare the plan invalid and shall order the commission to adopt a new general assembly district plan in accordance with this article.

(c) If, in considering a plan adopted under division (C) of Section 8 of this article, the court determines that both of the following are true, the court shall order the commission to adopt a new general assembly district plan in accordance with this article:

(i) The plan significantly violates those requirements in a manner that materially affects the ability of the plan to contain districts whose voters favor political parties in an overall proportion that corresponds closely to the statewide political party preferences of the voters of Ohio, as described in division (B) of Section 6 of this article.

(ii) The statewide proportion of districts in the plan whose voters, based on statewide state and federal partisan general election results during the last ten years, favor each political party does not correspond closely to the statewide preferences of the voters of Ohio.

Section 10. The various provisions of this article are intended to be severable, and the invalidity of one or more of such provisions shall not affect the validity of the remaining provisions.

ARTICLE XII: FINANCE AND TAXATION

Section 1. Poll Taxes Prohibited

No poll tax shall ever be levied in this state, or service required, which may be commuted in money or other thing of value.

Section 2. Limitation on Tax Rate; Exemption

No property, taxed according to value, shall be so taxed in excess of one per cent of its true value in money for all state and local purposes, but laws may be passed authorizing additional taxes to be levied outside of such limitation, either when approved by at least a majority of the electors of the taxing district voting on such proposition, or when provided for by the charter of a municipal corporation. Land and improvements thereon shall be taxed by uniform rule according to value, except that laws may be passed to reduce taxes by providing for a reduction in value of the homestead of permanently and totally disabled residents, residents sixty-five years of age and older, and residents sixty years of age or older who are surviving spouses of deceased residents who were sixtyfive years of age or older or permanently and totally disabled and receiving a reduction in the value of their homestead at the time of death, provided the surviving spouse continues to reside in a qualifying homestead, and providing for income and other qualifications to obtain such reduction. Without limiting the general power, subject to the provisions of Article I of this constitution, to determine the subjects and methods of taxation or exemptions therefrom, general laws may be passed to exempt burying grounds, public school houses, houses used exclusively for public worship, institutions used exclusively for charitable purposes, and public property used exclusively for any public purpose, but all such laws shall be subject to alteration or repeal; and the value of all property so exempted shall, from time to time, be ascertained and published as may be directed by law.

Section 2a. Authority to Classify Real Estate for Taxation; Procedures

(A) Except as expressly authorized in this section, land and improvements thereon shall, in all other respects, be taxed as provided in Section 36, of Article II and Section 2 of this article

(B) This section does not apply to any of the following:

(1) Taxes levied at whatever rate is required to produce a specified amount of tax money or an amount to pay debt charges;

(2) Taxes levied within the one per cent limitation imposed by Section 2 of this article;

(3) Taxes provided for by the charter of a municipal corporation.

(C) Notwithstanding Section 2 of this article, laws may be passed that provide all of the following:

(1) Land and improvements thereon in each taxing district shall be placed into one of two classes solely for the purpose of separately reducing the taxes charged against all land and improvements in each of the two classes as provided in division

(C)(2) of this section. The classes shall be:

(a) Residential and agricultural land and improvements;

(b) All other land and improvements.

(2) With respect to each voted tax authorized to be levied by each taxing district, the amount of taxes imposed by such tax against all land and improvements thereon in each class shall be reduced in order that the amount charged for collection against all land and improvements in that class in the current year, exclusive of land and improvements not taxed by the district in both the preceding year and in the current year and those not taxed in that class in the preceding year, equals the amount charged for collection against such land and improvements in the preceding year.

(D) Laws may be passed to provide that the reductions made under this section in the amounts of taxes charged for the current expenses of cities, townships, school districts, counties, or other taxing districts are subject to the limitation that the sum of the amounts of all taxes charged for current expenses against the land and improvements thereon in each of the two classes of property subject to taxation in cities, townships, school districts, counties, or other types of taxing districts, shall not be less than a uniform per cent of the taxable value of the property in the districts to which the limitation applies. Different but uniform percentage limitations may be established for cities, townships, school districts, counties, and other types of taxing districts.

Section 3. Imposition of Taxes

Laws may be passed providing for:

(A) The taxation of decedents' estates or of the right to receive or succeed to such estates, and the rates of such taxation may be uniform or may be graduated based on the value of the estate, inheritance, or succession. Such tax may also be levied at different rates upon collateral and direct inheritances, and a portion of each estate may be exempt from such taxation as provided by law.

(B) The taxation of incomes, and the rates of such taxation may be either uniform or graduated, and may be applied to such incomes and with such exemptions as may be provided by law.

(C) Excise and franchise taxes and for the imposition of taxes upon the production of coal, oil, gas, and other minerals; except that no excise tax shall be levied or collected upon the sale or purchase of food for human consumption off the premises where sold.

Section 4. Revenue to Pay Expenses and Retire Debts

The General Assembly shall provide for raising revenue, sufficient to defray the expenses of the state, for each year, and also a sufficient sum to pay principal and interest as they become due on the state debt.

Section 5. Levying of Taxes

No tax shall be levied, except in pursuance of law; and every law imposing a tax shall state, distinctly, the object of the same, to which only, it shall be applied.

Section 5a. Use of Motor Vehicle License and Fuel Taxes Restricted

No moneys derived from fees, excises, or license taxes relating to registration, operation, or use of vehicles on public highways, or to fuels used for propelling such vehicles, shall be expended for other than costs of administering such laws, statutory refunds and adjustments provided therein, payment of highway obligations, costs for construction, reconstruction, maintenance and repair of public highways and bridges and other statutory highway purposes, expense of state enforcement of traffic laws, and expenditures authorized for hospitalization of indigent persons injured in motor vehicle accidents on the public highways.

Section 6. No Debt for Internal Improvement

Except as otherwise provided in this constitution the state shall never contract any debt for purposes of internal improvement.

Section 7. Repealed

Section 8. Repealed

Section 9. Apportionment of Income, Estate, and Inheritance Taxes

Not less than fifty per cent of the income, estate, and inheritance taxes that may be collected by the state shall be returned to the county, school district, city, village, or township in which said income, estate, or inheritance tax originates, or to any of the same, as may be provided by law.

Section 10. Repealed

Section 11. Sinking Fund

No bonded indebtedness of the state, or any political subdivisions thereof, shall be incurred or renewed unless, in the legislation under which such indebtedness is incurred or renewed, provision is made for levying and collecting annually by taxation an amount sufficient to pay the interest on said bonds, and to provide a sinking fund for their final redemption at maturity.

Section 12. Repealed

Section 13. Wholesale Taxes on Foods

No sales or other excise taxes shall be levied or collected

(1) upon any wholesale sale or wholesale purchase of food for human consumption, its ingredients or its packaging,

(2) upon any sale or purchase of such items sold to or purchased by a manufacturer, processor, packager, distributor or reseller of food for human consumption, or its ingredients, for use in its trade or business; or

(3) in any retail transaction, on any packaging that contains food for human consumption on or off the premises where sold. For purposes of this section, food for human consumption shall include nonalcoholic beverages. This section shall not affect the extent to which the levy or collection of sales or other excise taxes on the retail sale or retail purchase of food for human consumption is permitted or prohibited by Section 3(C) of this Article.

ARTICLE XIII: CORPORATIONS

Section 1. Special Acts Conferring Corporate Powers; Prohibited

The General Assembly shall pass no special act conferring corporate powers.

Section 2. Corporations, How Formed

Corporations may be formed under general laws; but all such laws may, from time to time, be altered or repealed. Corporations may be classified and there may be conferred upon proper boards, commissions or officers, such supervisory and regulatory powers over their organization, business and issue and sale of stocks and securities and over the business and sale of the stocks and securities of foreign corporations and joint stock companies in this state, as may be prescribed by law. Laws may be passed regulating the sale and conveyance of other personal property, whether owned by a corporation, joint stock company or individual.

Section 3. Liability of Stockholders for Unpaid Subscriptions; Dues from Corporations; How Secured; Inspection of Private Banks

Dues from private corporations shall be secured by such means as may be prescribed by law, but in no case shall any stockholder be individually liable otherwise than for the unpaid stock owned by him or her. No corporation not organized under the laws of this state, or of the United States, or person, partnership or association shall use the word 'bank," "banker" or "banking," or words of similar meaning in any foreign language, as a designation or name under which business may be conducted in this state unless such corporation, person, partnership or association shall submit to inspection, examination and regulation as may hereafter be provided by the laws of this state.

Section 4. Corporate Property Subject to Taxation

The property of corporations, now existing or hereafter created, shall forever be subject to taxation, the same as the property of individuals.

Section 5. Corporate Power to Eminent Domain to Obtain Rights of Way; Procedure; Jury Trial

No right of way shall be appropriated to the use of any corporation, until full compensation therefore be first made in money or first secured by a deposit of money, to the owner, irrespective of any benefit from any improvement proposed by such corporation, which compensation shall be ascertained by a jury of twelve men, in a court of record, as shall be prescribed by law.

Section 6. Organization of Cities, Etc.

The General Assembly shall provide for the organization of cities, and incorporated villages, by general laws, and restrict their power of taxation, assessment, borrowing money, contracting debts and loaning their credit, so as to prevent the abuse of such power.

Section 7. Acts Authorizing Associations with Banking Powers; Referendum

No act of the General Assembly, authorizing associations with banking powers, shall take effect until it shall be submitted to the people, at the general election next succeeding the passage thereof, and be approved by a majority of all the electors, voting at such election.

ARTICLE XIV: AGRICULTURE

Section 1. Ohio Livestock Care Standards Board

(A) There is hereby created the Ohio Livestock Care Standards Board for the purpose of establishing standards governing the care and well-being of livestock and poultry in this state. In carrying out its purpose, the Board shall endeavor to maintain food safety, encourage locally grown and raised food, and protect Ohio farms and families. The Board shall be comprised of the following thirteen members:

(1) The director of the state department that regulates agriculture who shall be the chairperson of the Board;

(2) Ten members appointed by the Governor with the advice and consent of the Senate. The ten members appointed by the Governor shall be residents of this state and shall include the following:

(a) One member representing family farms;

(b) One member who is knowledgeable about food safety in this state;

(c) Two members representing statewide organizations that represent farmers;

(d) One member who is a veterinarian who is licensed in this state;

(e) The State Veterinarian in the state department that regulates agriculture;

(f) The dean of the agriculture department of a college or university located in this state;

(g) Two members of the public representing Ohio consumers;

(h) One member representing a county humane society that is organized under state law.

(3) One member appointed by the Speaker of the House of Representatives who shall be a family farmer;

(4) One member appointed by the President of the Senate who shall be a family farmer.
Not more than seven members appointed to the Board at any given time shall be of the same political party.

(B) The Board shall have authority to establish standards governing the care and well-being of livestock and poultry in this state, subject to the authority of the General Assembly. In establishing those standards, the Board shall consider factors that include, but are not limited to, agricultural best management practices for such care and well-being, biosecurity, disease prevention, animal morbidity and mortality data, food safety practices, and the protection of local, affordable food supplies for consumers.

(C) The state department that regulates agriculture shall have the authority to administer and enforce the standards established by the Board.

(D) The General Assembly may enact laws that it deems necessary to carry out the purposes of this section, to facilitate the execution of the duties of the Board and the state department that regulates agriculture under this section, and to set the terms of office of the Board members and conditions for the Board members' service on the Board.

(E) If any part of this section is held invalid, the remainder of this section shall not be affected by that holding and shall continue in full force and effect.

ARTICLE XV: MISCELLANEOUS

Section 1. Seat of Government

Columbus shall be the seat of government, until otherwise directed by law.

Section 2. Repealed

Section 3. Receipts and Expenditures; Publication of State Financial Statements

An accurate and detailed statement of the receipts and expenditures of the public money, the several amounts paid, to whom, and on what account, shall, from time to time, be published, as shall be prescribed by law.

Section 4. Officers to Be Qualified Electors

No person shall be elected or appointed to any office in this state unless possessed of the qualifications of an elector.

Section 5. Repealed

Section 6. Lotteries, Charitable Bingo

Except as otherwise provided in this section, lotteries, and the sale of lottery tickets, for any purpose whatever, shall forever be prohibited in this State.

(A) The General Assembly may authorize an agency of the state to conduct lotteries, to sell rights to participate therein, and to award prizes by chance to participants, provided that the entire net proceeds of any such lottery are paid into a fund of the state treasury that shall consist solely of such proceeds and shall be used solely for the support of elementary, secondary, vocational, and special education programs as determined in appropriations made by the General Assembly.

(B) The General Assembly may authorize and regulate the operation of bingo to be conducted by charitable organizations for charitable purposes.

(C)(1) Casino gaming shall be authorized at four casino facilities (a single casino at a designated location within each of the cities of Cincinnati, Cleveland, Columbus and Toledo) to create new funding for cities, counties, public school districts, law enforcement, the horse racing industry and job training for Ohio's workforce.

(2) A thirty-three percent tax shall be levied and collected by the state on all gross casino revenue received by each casino operator of these four casino facilities. In addition, casino operators, their operations, their owners, and their property shall be subject to all customary non-discriminatory fees, taxes, and other charges that are applied to, levied against, or otherwise imposed generally upon other Ohio businesses, their gross or net revenues, their operations, their owners, and their property. Except as otherwise provided in section 6(C), no other casino gaming-related state or local fees, taxes, or other charges (however measured, calculated, or otherwise derived) may be, directly or indirectly, applied to, levied against, or otherwise imposed upon gross casino revenue, casino operators, their operations, their owners, or their property.

(3) The proceeds of the tax on gross casino revenue collected by the state shall be distributed as follows:

(a) Fifty-one percent of the tax on gross casino revenue shall be distributed among all eighty-eight counties in proportion to such counties' respective populations at the time of such distribution. If a county's most populated city, as of the 2000 United States census bureau census, had a population greater than 80,000, then fifty percent of that county's distribution will go to said city.

(b) Thirty-four percent of the tax on gross casino revenue shall be distributed among all eighty-eight counties in proportion to such counties' respective public school district student populations at the time of such distribution. Each such distribution received by a county shall be distributed among all public school districts located (in whole or in part) within such county in proportion to each school district's respective student population who are residents of such county at the time of such distribution to the school districts. Each public school district shall determine how its distributions are appropriated, but all distributions shall only be used to support primary and secondary education.

(c) Five percent of the tax on gross casino revenue shall be distributed to the host city where the casino facility that generated such gross casino revenue is located.

(d) Three percent of the tax on gross casino revenue shall be distributed to fund the Ohio casino control commission.

(e) Three percent of the tax on gross casino revenue shall be distributed to an Ohio state racing commission fund to support purses, breeding programs, and operations at all existing commercial horse racetracks permitted as of January 1, 2009. However, no funding under this division shall be distributed to operations of an Ohio commercial horse racetrack if an owner or operator of the racetrack holds a majority interest in an Ohio casino facility or in an Ohio casino license.

(f) Two percent of the tax on gross casino revenue shall be distributed to a state law enforcement training fund to enhance public safety by providing additional training opportunities to the law enforcement community.

(g) Two percent of the tax on gross casino revenue shall be distributed to a state problem gambling and addictions fund which shall be used for the treatment of problem gambling and substance abuse, and related research.

Tax collection, and distributions to public school districts and local governments, under sections 6(C)(2) and (3), are intended to supplement, not supplant, any funding obligations of the state. Accordingly, all such distributions shall be disregarded for purposes of determining whether funding obligations imposed by other sections of this Constitution are met.

(4) There is hereby created the Ohio casino control commission which shall license and regulate casino operators, management companies retained by such casino operators, key employees of such casino operators and such management companies, gaming related vendors, and all gaming authorized by section 6(C), to ensure the integrity of casino gaming.

Said commission shall determine all voting issues by majority vote and shall consist of seven members appointed by the governor with the advice and consent of the senate. Each member of the commission must be a resident of Ohio. At least one member of the commission must be experienced in law enforcement and criminal investigation. At least one member of the commission must be a certified public accountant experienced in accounting and auditing. At least one member of the commission must be an attorney admitted to the practice of law in Ohio. At least one member of the commission must be a resident of a county where one of the casino facilities is located. Not more than four members may be affiliated with the same political party. No commission member may have any affiliation with an Ohio casino operator or facility.

Said commission shall require each initial licensed casino operator of each of the four casino facilities to pay an upfront license fee of fifty million dollars ($50,000,000) per casino facility for the benefit of the state, for a total of two hundred million dollars ($200,000,000). The upfront license fee shall be used to fund state economic development programs which support regional job training efforts to equip Ohio's workforce with additional skills to grow the economy.

To carry out the tax provisions of section 6(C), and in addition to any other enforcement powers provided under Ohio law, the tax commissioner of the State and the Ohio casino control commission, or any person employed by the tax commissioner or said commission for that purpose, upon demand, may inspect books, accounts, records, and memorandum of any person subject to such provisions, and may examine under oath any officer, agent, or employee of that person.

(5) Each initial licensed casino operator of each of the four casino facilities shall make an initial investment of at least two hundred fifty million dollars ($250,000,000) for the development of each casino facility for a total minimum investment of one billion dollars ($1,000,000,000) statewide. A casino operator: (a) may not hold a majority interest in more than two of the four licenses allocated to the casino facilities at any one time; and (b) may not hold a majority interest in more than two of the four casino facilities at any one time.

(6) Casino gaming authorized in section 6(C) shall be conducted only by licensed casino operators of the four casino facilities or by licensed management companies retained by such casino operators. At the discretion of each licensed casino operator of a casino facility: (a) casino gaming may be conducted twenty-four hours each day; and (b) a maximum of five thousand slot machines may be operated at such casino facility.

(7) Each of the four casino facilities shall be subject to all applicable state laws and local ordinances related to health and building codes, or any related requirements and provisions. Notwithstanding the foregoing, no local zoning, land use laws, subdivision regulations or similar provisions shall prohibit the development or operation of the four casino facilities set forth herein, provided that no casino facility shall be located in a district zoned exclusively residential as of January 1, 2009.

(8) Notwithstanding any provision of the Constitution, statutes of Ohio, or a local charter and ordinance, only one casino facility shall be operated in each of the cities of Cleveland, Columbus, Cincinnati and Toledo.

(9) For purposes of this section 6(C), the following definitions shall be applied:
"Casino facility" means all or any part of any one or more of the following properties (together with all improvements situated thereon) in Cleveland, Cincinnati, Columbus and Toledo:

(a) Cleveland:

Being an approximate 61 acre area in Cuyahoga County, Ohio, as identified by the Cuyahoga County Auditor, as of 02/27/09, as tax parcel numbers 004-28-001, 004-29-004A, 004- 29-005, 004-29-008, 004-29-009, 004-29-010, 004-29-012, 004-29-013, 004-29-014, 004-29-020, 004-29-018, 004-29-017, 004-29-016, 004-29-021, 004-29-025, 004-29-027, 004-29-026, 004-28-008, 004-28-004, 004-28-003, 004-28-002, 004-28-010, 004-29-001, 004-29-007 and 004-04-017 and all lands and air rights lying within and/or above the public rights of way adjacent to such parcels.

Being an approximate 8.66 acre area in Cuyahoga County, Ohio, being that parcel identified by the Cuyahoga County Auditor, as of 02/27/09, as tax parcel number 101-21-002 and all lands and air rights lying within and/or above the public rights of way adjacent to such parcel.

Being an approximate 2.56 acre area in Cuyahoga County, Ohio, being that parcel identified by the Cuyahoga County Auditor, as of 02/27/09, as tax parcel number 101-21-002 and all lands and air rights lying within and/or above the public rights of way adjacent to such parcel.

Being an approximate 7.91 acre area in Cuyahoga County, Ohio, being that parcel identified by the Cuyahoga County Auditor, as of 02/27/09, as tax parcel number 101-23-050A and all lands and air rights lying within and/or above the public rights of way adjacent to such parcel.

All air rights above the parcel located in Cuyahoga County, Ohio identified by the Cuyahoga County Auditor, as of 02/27/09, as tax parcel number 101-22-003.

Being an approximate 1.55 acre area in Cuyahoga County, Ohio, as identified by the Cuyahoga County Auditor, as of 02/27/09, as tax parcel numbers 122-18-010, 122-18-011 and 122-18-012 and all lands and air rights lying within and/or above the public rights of way adjacent to such parcels.

Being an approximate 1.83 acre area in Cuyahoga County, Ohio, as identified by the Cuyahoga County Auditor, as of 02/27/09, as tax parcel numbers 101-30-002 and 101-30- 003 and all lands and air rights lying within and/or above the public rights of way adjacent to such parcels.

Consisting of floors one through four, mezzanine, basement, sub-basement, Parcel No. 36-2, Item III, Parcels First and Second, Item V, Parcel A, and Item VI, Parcel One of the Higbee Building in Cuyahoga County, Ohio, as identified by the Cuyahoga County Auditor, as of 2/29/09, as tax parcel numbers 101-23-002 and 101-23- 050F and all lands and air rights lying within and/or above the public rights of way adjacent to such parcels.

(b) Franklin County:
Being an approximate 113.794 acre area in Franklin County, Ohio, as identified by the Franklin County Auditor, as of 01/19/10, as tax parcel number 140-003620-00.

(c) Cincinnati:

Being an approximate 20.4 acre area in Hamilton County, Ohio, being identified by the Hamilton County Auditor, as of 02/27/09, as tax parcel numbers 074-0002-0009-00, 074- 0001-0001-00, 074-0001-0002-00, 074-0001-0003-00, 074-0001-0004- 00, 074-

0001-0006-00, 074-0001- 0008-00, 074-0001-0014-00, 074-0001-0016-00, 074-0001-0031- 00, 074-0001-0039-00, 074-0001- 0041-00, 074-0001-0042-00, 074- 0001-0043-00, 074-0002-0001-00, 074-0004-0001-00, 074-0004-0002- 00, 074-0004-0003-00 and 074-0005- 0003-00.

(d) Toledo:

Being an approximate 44.24 acre area in the City of Toledo, Lucas County, Ohio, as identified by the Lucas County Auditor, as of 03/05/09, as tax parcel numbers 18-76138 and 18-76515. "Casino gaming" means any type of slot machine or table game wagering, using money, casino credit, or any representative of value, authorized in any of the states of Indiana, Michigan, Pennsylvania and West Virginia as of January 1, 2009, and shall include slot machine and table game wagering subsequently authorized by, but shall not be limited by subsequent restrictions placed on such wagering in, such states. Notwithstanding the aforementioned definition, "casino gaming" does not include bingo, as authorized in article XV, section 6 of the Ohio Constitution and conducted as of January 1, 2009, or horse racing where the pari-mutuel system of wagering is conducted, as authorized under the laws of Ohio as of January 1, 2009. "Casino operator" means any person, trust, corporation, partnership, limited partnership, association, limited liability company or other business enterprise that directly holds an ownership or leasehold interest in a casino facility. "Casino operator" does not include an agency of the state, any political subdivision of the state, or any person, trust, corporation, partnership, limited partnership, association, limited liability company or other business enterprise that may have an interest in a casino facility, but who is legally or contractually restricted from conducting casino gaming.

"Gross casino revenue" means the total amount of money exchanged for the purchase of chips, tokens, tickets, electronic cards, or similar objects by casino patrons, less winnings paid to wagerers.

"Majority interest" in a license or in a casino facility (as the case may be) means beneficial ownership of more than fifty percent (50%) of the total fair market value of such license or casino facility (as the case may be). For purposes of the foregoing, whether a majority interest is held in a license or in a casino facility (as the case may be) shall be determined in accordance with the rules for constructive ownership of stock provided in Treas. Reg. § 1.409A-3(i)(5)(iii) as in effect on January 1, 2009.
"Slot machines" shall include any mechanical, electrical, or other device or machine which, upon insertion of a coin, token, ticket, or similar object, or upon payment of any consideration, is available to play or operate, the play or operation of which, whether by reason of the skill of the operator or application of the element of chance, or both, makes individual prize determinations for individual participants in cash, premiums, merchandise, tokens, or any thing of value, whether the payoff is made automatically from the machine or in any other manner.
"Table game" means any game played with cards, dice, or any mechanical, electromechanical, or electronic device or machine for money, casino credit, or any representative of value.

(10) The General Assembly shall pass laws within six months of the effective date of section 6(C) to facilitate the operation of section 6(C).

(11) Each provision of section 6(C) is intended to be independent and severable, and if any provision of section 6(C) is held to be invalid, either on its face or as applied to any person or circumstance, the remaining provisions of section 6(C), and the application thereof to any person or circumstance other than those to which it is held invalid, shall not be affected thereby. In any case of a conflict between any provision of section 6(C) and any other provision contained in this Constitution, the provisions of section 6(C) shall control.

(12) Notwithstanding the provisions of section 6(C)(11), nothing in this section 6(C) (including, without limitation, the provisions of sections 6(C)(6) and 6(C)(8)) shall restrict or in any way limit lotteries authorized under section 6(A) of this article or bingo authorized under section 6(B) of this article. The provisions of this section 6(C) shall have no effect upon activities authorized under sections 6(A) and / or (6)(B) of this article.

Section 7. Oath of Officers

Every person chosen or appointed to any office under this state, before entering upon the discharge of its duties, shall take an oath or affirmation, to support the Constitution of the United States, and of this state, and also an oath of office.

Section 8. Repealed

Section 9. Repealed

Section 9a. Repealed

Section 10. Civil Service

Appointments and promotions in the civil service of the state, the several counties, and cities, shall be made according to merit and fitness, to be ascertained, as is practicable, by competitive examinations. Laws shall be passed providing for the enforcement of this provision.

Section 11. Marriage

Only a union between one man and one woman may be a marriage valid in or recognized by this state and its political subdivisions. This state and its political subdivisions shall not create or recognize a legal status for relationships of unmarried individuals that intends to approximate the design, qualities, significance or effect of marriage.

ARTICLE XVI: AMENDMENTS

Section 1. How Constitution to Be Amended; Ballot; Supreme Court to Hear Challenges

Either branch of the General Assembly may propose amendments to this constitution; and, if the same shall be agreed to by three-fifths of the members elected to each house, such proposed amendments shall be entered on the journals, with the yeas and nays, and shall be filed with the secretary of state at least ninety days before the date of the election at which they are to be submitted to the electors, for their approval or rejection. They shall be submitted on a separate ballot without party designation of any kind, at either a special or a general election as the General Assembly may prescribe.

The ballot language for such proposed amendments shall be prescribed by a majority of the Ohio ballot board, consisting of the secretary of state and four other members, who shall be designated in a manner prescribed by law and not more than two of whom shall be members of the same political party. The ballot language shall properly identify the substance of the proposal to be voted upon. The ballot need not contain the full text nor a condensed text of the proposal. The board shall also prepare an explanation of the proposal, which may include its purpose and effects, and shall certify the ballot language and the explanation to the secretary of state not later than seventy-five days before the election. The ballot language and the explanation shall be available for public inspection in the office of the secretary of state.

The Supreme Court shall have exclusive, original jurisdiction in all cases challenging the adoption or submission of a proposed constitutional amendment to the electors. No such case challenging the ballot language, the explanation, or the actions or procedures of the General Assembly in adopting and submitting a constitutional amendment shall be filed later than sixty-four days before the election. The ballot language shall not be held invalid unless it is such as to mislead, deceive, or defraud the voters.

Unless the General Assembly otherwise provides by law for the preparation of arguments for and, if any, against a proposed amendment, the board may prepare such arguments.
Such proposed amendments, the ballot language, the explanations, and the arguments, if any, shall be published once a week for three consecutive weeks preceding such election, in at least one newspaper of general circulation in each county of the state, where a newspaper is published. The General Assembly shall provide by law for other dissemination of information in order to inform the electors concerning proposed amendments. An election on a proposed constitutional amendment submitted by the general assembly shall not be enjoined nor invalidated because the explanation, arguments, or other information is faulty in any way. If the majority of the electors voting on the same shall adopt such amendments the same shall become a part of the constitution. When more than one amendment shall be submitted at the same time, they shall be so submitted as to enable the electors to vote on each amendment, separately.

Section 2. Convention

Whenever two-thirds of the members elected to each branch of the General Assembly shall think it necessary to call a convention, to revise, amend, or change this constitution, they shall recommend to the electors to vote on a separate ballot without party designation of any kind at the next election for members to the general assembly, for or against a convention; and if a majority of all the electors, voting for and against the calling of a convention, shall have voted for a convention, the General Assembly shall, at their next session, provide, by law, for calling the same. Candidates for members of the constitutional convention shall be nominated by nominating petitions only and shall be voted for upon one independent and separate ballot without any emblem or party designation whatever. The convention shall consist of as many members as the House of Representatives, who shall be chosen as provided by law, and shall meet within three months after their election, for the purpose, aforesaid.

Section 3. Question of Constitutional Convention to Be Submitted Periodically

At the general election to be held in the year one thousand nine hundred and thirty-two, and in each twentieth year thereafter, the question: "Shall there be a convention to revise, alter, or amend the constitution," shall be submitted to the electors of the state; and in case a majority of the electors, voting for and against the calling of a convention, shall decide in favor of a convention, the General Assembly, at its next session, shall provide, by law, for the election of delegates, and the assembling of such convention, as is provided in the preceding section; but no amendment of this constitution, agreed upon by any convention assembled in pursuance of this article, shall take effect, until the same shall have been submitted to the electors of the state, and adopted by a majority of those voting thereon.

ARTICLE XVII: ELECTIONS

Section 1. Time for Holding

Elections for state and county officers shall be held on the first Tuesday after the first Monday in November in even numbered years; and all elections for all other elective officers shall be held on the first Tuesday after the first Monday in November in the odd numbered years.

The term of office of all elective county, township, municipal, and school officers shall be such even number of years not exceeding four as may be prescribed by law or such even number of years as may be provided in municipal or county charters.

The term of office of all judges shall be as provided in Article IV of this constitution or, if not so provided, an even number of years not exceeding six as provided by law.

The General Assembly may extend existing terms of office as to effect the purpose of this section.

Section 2. Terms of Officers, Vacancies, Etc

Any vacancy which may occur in any elective state office created by Article II or III or created by or pursuant to Article IV of this constitution shall be filled only if and as provided in such articles. Any vacancy which may occur in any elective state office not so created, shall be filled by appointment by the Governor until the disability is removed, or a successor elected and qualified. Such successor shall be elected for the unexpired term of the vacant office at the first general election in an even numbered year that occurs more than forty days after the vacancy has occurred; provided, that when the unexpired term ends within one year immediately following the date of such general election, an election to fill such unexpired term shall not be held and the appointment shall be for such unexpired term. All vacancies in other elective offices shall be filled for the unexpired term in such manner as may be prescribed by this constitution or by law.

Section 3. Repealed

ARTICLE XVIII: MUNICIPAL CORPORATIONS

Section 1. Classification

Municipal corporations are hereby classified into cities and villages. All such corporations having a population of five thousand or over shall be cities; all others shall be villages. The method of transition from one class to the other shall be regulated by law.

Section 2. General and Additional Laws

General laws shall be passed to provide for the incorporation and government of cities and villages; and additional laws may also be passed for the government of municipalities adopting the same; but no such additional law shall become operative in any municipality until it shall have been submitted to the electors thereof, and affirmed by a majority of those voting thereon, under regulations to be established by law.

Section 3. Powers

Municipalities shall have authority to exercise all powers of local self-government and to adopt and enforce within their limits such local police, sanitary and other similar regulations, as are not in conflict with general laws.

Section 4. Acquisition of Public Utility; Contract for Service; Condemnation

Any municipality may acquire, construct, own, lease and operate within or without its corporate limits, any public utility the product or service of which is or is to be supplied to the municipality or its inhabitants, and may contract with others for any such product or service. The acquisition of any such public utility may be by condemnation or otherwise, and a municipality may acquire thereby the use of, or full title to, the property and franchise of any company or person supplying to the municipality or its inhabitants the service or product of any such utility.

Section 5. Acquisition by Ordinance; Procedure; Referendum; Submission

Any municipality proceeding to acquire, construct, own, lease or operate a public utility, or to contract with any person or company therefore, shall act by ordinance and no such ordinance shall take effect until after thirty days from its passage. If within said thirty days a petition signed by ten per centum of the electors of the municipality shall be filed with the executive authority thereof demanding a referendum on such ordinance it shall not take effect until submitted to the electors and approved by a majority of those voting thereon. The submission of any such question shall be governed by all the provisions of section 8 of this article as to the submission of the question of choosing a charter commission.

Section 6. Sale of Surplus

Any municipality, owning or operating a public utility for the purpose of supplying the service or product thereof to the municipality or its inhabitants, may also sell and deliver to others any transportation service of such utility and the surplus product of any other utility in an amount not exceeding in either case fifty per cent of the total service or product supplied by such utility within the municipality, provided that such fifty per cent limitation shall not apply to the sale of water or sewage services.

Section 7. Home Rule

Any municipality may frame and adopt or amend a charter for its government and may, subject to the provisions of section 3 of this article, exercise thereunder all powers of local self-government.

Section 8. Submission of Question of Election of Charter Commission; Approval

The legislative authority of any city or village may by a two-thirds vote of its members, and upon petition of ten per centum of the electors shall forthwith, provide by ordinance for the submission to the electors, of the question, "Shall a commission be chosen to frame a charter." The ordinance providing for the submission of such question shall require that it be submitted to the electors at the next regular municipal election if one shall occur not less than sixty nor more than one hundred and twenty days after its passage; otherwise it shall provide for the submission of the question at a special election to be called and held within the time aforesaid. The ballot containing such question shall bear no party designation, and provision shall be made thereon for the election from the municipality at large of fifteen electors who shall constitute a commission to frame a charter; provided that a majority of the electors voting on such question shall have voted in the affirmative. Any charter so framed shall be submitted to the electors of the municipality at an election to be held at a time fixed by the charter commission and within one year from the date of its election, provision for which shall be made by the legislative authority of the municipality in so far as not prescribed by general law. Not less than thirty days prior to such election the clerk of the municipality shall mail a copy of the proposed charter to each elector whose name appears upon the poll or registration books of the last regular or general election held therein. If such proposed charter is approved by a majority of the electors voting thereon it shall become the charter of such municipality at the time fixed therein.

Section 9. Amendments to Charter; Submission; Approval

Amendments to any charter framed and adopted as herein provided may be submitted to the electors of a municipality by a two-thirds vote of the legislative authority thereof, and, upon petitions signed by ten per centum of the electors of the municipality setting forth any such proposed amendment, shall be submitted by such legislative authority. The submission of proposed amendments to the electors shall be governed by the requirements of section 8 as to the submission of the question of choosing a charter commission; and copies of proposed amendments may be mailed to the electors as hereinbefore provided for copies of a proposed charter, or pursuant to laws passed by the general assembly, notice of proposed amendments may be given by newspaper advertising. If any such amendment is approved by a majority of the electors voting thereon, it shall become a part of the charter of the municipality. A copy of said charter or any amendment thereto shall be certified to the secretary of state, within thirty days after adoption by a referendum vote.

Section 10. Appropriation in Excess of Public Use

A municipality appropriating or otherwise acquiring property for public use may in furtherance of such public use appropriate or acquire an excess over that actually to be occupied by the improvement, and may sell such excess with such restrictions as shall be appropriate to preserve the improvement made. Bonds may be issued to supply the funds in whole or in part to pay for the excess property so appropriated or otherwise acquired, but said bonds shall be a lien only against the property so acquired for the improvement and excess, and they shall not be a liability of the municipality nor be included in any limitation of the bonded indebtedness of such municipality prescribed by law.

Section 11. Assessments for Cost of Appropriating Property

Any municipality appropriating private property for a public improvement may provide money therefore in part by assessments upon benefited property not in excess of the special benefits conferred upon such property by the improvements. Said assessments, however, upon all the abutting, adjacent, and other property in the district benefited, shall in no case be levied for more than fifty per centum of the cost of such appropriation.

Section 12. Bonds for Public Utilities

Any municipality which acquires, constructs or extends any public utility and desires to raise money for such purposes may issue mortgage bonds therefore beyond the general limit of bonded indebtedness prescribed by law; provided that such mortgage bonds issued beyond the general limit of bonded indebtedness prescribed by law shall not impose any liability upon such municipality but shall be secured only upon the property and revenues of such public utility, including a franchise stating the terms upon which, in case of foreclosure, the purchaser may operate the same, which franchise shall in no case extend for a longer period than twenty years from the date of the sale of such utility and franchise on foreclosure.

Section 13. Taxation, Debts, Reports, and Accounts

Laws may be passed to limit the power of municipalities to levy taxes and incur debts for local purposes, and may require reports from municipalities as to their financial condition and transactions, in such form as may be provided by law, and may provide for the examination of the vouchers, books and accounts of all municipal authorities, or of public undertakings conducted by such authorities.

Section 14. Elections

All elections and submissions of questions provided for in this article shall be conducted by the election authorities prescribed by general law. The percentage of electors required to sign any petition provided for herein shall be based upon the total vote cast at the last preceding general municipal election.

ARTICLE XIX: CONGRESSIONAL REDISTRICTING

Section 1.

(A) Except as otherwise provided in this section, the general assembly shall be responsible for the redistricting of this state for congress based on the prescribed number of congressional districts apportioned to the state pursuant to Section 2 of Article I of the Constitution of the United States.
Not later than the last day of September of a year ending in the numeral one, the general assembly shall pass a congressional district plan in the form of a bill by the affirmative vote of three-fifths of the members of each house of the general assembly, including the affirmative vote of at least one-half of the members of each of the two largest political parties represented in that house. A congressional district plan that is passed under this division and becomes law shall remain effective until the next year ending in the numeral one, except as provided in Section 3 of this article.

(B) If a congressional district plan is not passed not later than the last day of September of a year ending in the numeral one and filed with the secretary of state in accordance with Section 16 of Article II of this constitution, then the Ohio redistricting commission described in Article XI of this constitution shall adopt a congressional district plan not later than the last day of October of that year by the affirmative vote of four members of the commission, including at least two members of the commission who represent each of the two largest political parties represented in the general assembly. The plan shall take effect upon filing with the secretary of state and shall remain effective until the next year ending in the numeral one, except as provided in Section 3 of this article.

(C) (1) If the Ohio redistricting commission does not adopt a plan not later than the last day of October of a year ending in the numeral one, then the general assembly shall pass a congressional district plan in the form of a bill not later than the last day of November of that year.

(2) If the general assembly passes a congressional district plan under division (C)(1) of this section by the affirmative vote of three-fifths of the members of each house of the general assembly, including the affirmative vote of at least one-third of the members of each of the two largest political parties represented in that house, and the plan becomes law, the plan shall remain effective until the next year ending in the numeral one, except as provided in Section 3 of this article.

(3) If the general assembly passes a congressional district plan under division (C)(1) of this section by a simple majority of the members of each house of the general assembly, and not by the vote described in division (C)(2) of this section, all of the following shall apply:

(a) The general assembly shall not pass a plan that unduly favors or disfavors a political party or its incumbents.

(b) The general assembly shall not unduly split governmental units, giving preference to keeping whole, in the order named, counties, then townships and municipal corporations.

(c) Division (B)(2) of Section 2 of this article shall not apply to the plan. The general assembly shall attempt to draw districts that are compact.

(d) The general assembly shall include in the plan an explanation of the plan's compliance with divisions (C)(3)(a) to (c) of this section.

(e) If the plan becomes law, the plan shall remain effective until two general elections for the United States house of representatives have occurred under the plan, except as provided in Section 3 of this article.

(D) Not later than the last day of September of the year after the year in which a plan expires under division (C)(3)(e) of this section, the general assembly shall pass a congressional district plan in the form of a bill by the affirmative vote of three-fifths of the members of each house of the general assembly, including the affirmative vote of at least one-half of the members of each of the two largest political parties represented in that house. A congressional district plan that is passed under this division and becomes law shall remain effective until the next year ending in the numeral one, except as provided in Section 3 of this article.

(E) If a congressional district plan is not passed not later than the last day of September of the year after the year in which a plan expires under division (C)(3)(e) of this section and filed with the secretary of state in accordance with Section 16 of Article II of this constitution, then the Ohio redistricting commission described in Article XI of this constitution shall be reconstituted and reconvene and shall adopt a congressional district plan not later than the last day of October of that year by the affirmative vote of four members of the commission, including at least two members of the commission who represent each of the two largest political parties represented in the general assembly. A congressional district plan adopted under this division shall take effect upon filing with the secretary of state and shall remain effective until the next year ending in the numeral one, except as provided in Section 3 of this article.
A congressional district plan passed under this division shall be drawn using the federal decennial census data or other data on which the previous redistricting was based.

(F) (1) If the Ohio redistricting commission does not adopt a congressional district plan not later than the last day of October of the year after the year in which a plan expires under division (C)(3)(e) of this section, then the general assembly shall pass a congressional district plan in the form of a bill not later than the last day of November of that year.

A congressional district plan adopted under this division shall be drawn using the federal decennial census data or other data on which the previous redistricting was based.

(2) If the general assembly passes a congressional district plan under division (F)(1) of this section by the affirmative vote of three-fifths of the members of each house, including the affirmative vote of at least one-third of the members of each of the two largest political parties represented in that house, and the plan becomes law, it shall remain effective until the next year ending in the numeral one, except as provided in Section 3 of this article.

(3) If the general assembly passes a congressional district plan under division (F)(1) of this section by a simple majority vote of the members of each house of the general assembly, and not by the vote described in division (F)(2) of this section, all of the following shall apply:

(a) The general assembly shall not pass a plan that unduly favors or disfavors a political party or its incumbents.

(b) The general assembly shall not unduly split governmental units, giving preference to keeping whole, in the order named, counties, then townships and municipal corporations.

(c) Division (B)(2) of Section 2 of this article shall not apply to the plan. The general assembly shall attempt to draw districts that are compact.

(d) The general assembly shall include in the plan an explanation of the plan's compliance with divisions (F)(3)(a) to (c) of this section.

(e) If the plan becomes law, the plan shall remain effective until the next year ending in the numeral one, except as provided in Section 3 of this article.

(G) Before the general assembly passes a congressional district plan under any division of this section, a joint committee of the general assembly shall hold at least two public committee hearings concerning a proposed plan. Before the Ohio redistricting commission adopts a congressional district plan under any division of this section, the commission shall hold at least two public hearings concerning a proposed plan.

(H) The general assembly and the Ohio redistricting commission shall facilitate and allow for the submission of proposed congressional district plans by members of the public. The general assembly shall provide by law the manner in which members of the public may do so.

(I) For purposes of filing a congressional district plan with the governor or the secretary of state under this article, a congressional district plan shall include both a legal description of the boundaries of the congressional districts and all electronic data necessary to create a congressional district map for the purpose of holding congressional elections.

(J) When a congressional district plan ceases to be effective under this article, the district boundaries described in that plan shall continue in operation for the purpose of holding elections until a new congressional district plan takes effect in accordance with this article. If a vacancy occurs in a district that was created under the previous district plan, the election to fill the vacancy for the remainder of the unexpired term shall be held using the previous district plan.

Section 2.

(A) (1) Each congressional district shall be entitled to a single representative in the United States house of representatives in each congress.

(2) The whole population of the state, as determined by the federal decennial census or, if the federal decennial census is unavailable, another basis as directed by the general assembly, shall be divided by the number of congressional districts apportioned to the state pursuant to Section 2 of Article I of the Constitution of the United States, and the quotient shall be the congressional ratio of representation for the next ten years.

(3) Notwithstanding the fact that boundaries of counties, municipal corporations, and townships within a district may be changed, district boundaries shall be created by using the data from the most recent federal decennial census or from the basis directed by the general assembly, as applicable.

(B) A congressional district plan shall comply with all of the following requirements:

(1) The plan shall comply with all applicable provisions of the constitutions of Ohio and the United States and of federal law, including federal laws protecting racial minority voting rights.

(2) Every congressional district shall be compact.

(3) Every congressional district shall be composed of contiguous territory, and the boundary of each district shall be a single non-intersecting continuous line.

(4) Except as otherwise required by federal law, in a county that contains a population that exceeds the congressional ratio of representation, the authority drawing the districts shall take the first of the following actions that applies to that county:

(a) If a municipal corporation or township located in that county contains a population that exceeds the congressional ratio of representation, the authority shall attempt to include a significant portion of that municipal corporation or township in a single district and may include in that district other municipal corporations or townships that are located in that county and whose residents have similar interests as the residents of the municipal corporation or township that contains a population that exceeds the congressional ratio of representation. In determining whether the population of a municipal corporation or township exceeds the congressional ratio of representation for the purpose of this division, if the territory of that municipal corporation or township completely surrounds the territory of another municipal corporation or township, the territory of the surrounded municipal corporation or township shall be considered part of the territory of the surrounding municipal corporation or township.

(b) If one municipal corporation or township in that county contains a population of not less than one hundred thousand and not more than the congressional ratio of representation, that municipal corporation or township shall not be split. If that county contains two or more such municipal corporations or townships, only the most populous of those municipal corporations or townships shall not be split.

(5) Of the eighty-eight counties in this state, sixty-five counties shall be contained entirely within a district, eighteen counties may be split not more than once, and five counties may be split not more than twice. The authority drawing the districts may determine which counties may be split.

(6) If a congressional district includes only part of the territory of a particular county, the part of that congressional district that lies in that particular county shall be contiguous within the boundaries of the county.

(7) No two congressional districts shall share portions of the territory of more than one county, except for a county whose population exceeds four hundred thousand.

(8) The authority drawing the districts shall attempt to include at least one whole county in each congressional district. This division does not apply to a congressional district that is contained entirely within one county or that cannot be drawn in that manner while complying with federal law.

(C) (1) Except as otherwise provided in division (C)(2) of this section, for purposes of this article, a county, municipal corporation, or township is considered to be split if, based on the census data used for the purpose of redistricting, any contiguous portion of its territory is not contained entirely within one district.

(2) If a municipal corporation or township has territory in more than one county, the contiguous portion of that municipal corporation or township that lies in each county shall be considered to be a separate municipal corporation or township for purposes of this section.

Section 3.

(A) The supreme court of Ohio shall have exclusive, original jurisdiction in all cases arising under this article.

(B) (1) In the event that any section of this constitution relating to congressional redistricting, any congressional district plan, or any congressional district or group of congressional districts is challenged and is determined to be invalid by an un-appealed final order of a court of competent jurisdiction then, notwithstanding any other provisions of this constitution, the general assembly shall pass a congressional district plan in accordance with the provisions of this constitution that are then valid, to be used until the next time for redistricting under this article in accordance with the provisions of this constitution that are then valid.

The general assembly shall pass that plan not later than the thirtieth day after the last day on which an appeal of the court order could have been filed or, if the order is not appealable, the thirtieth day after the day on which the order is issued.
A congressional district plan passed under this division shall remedy any legal defects in the previous plan identified by the court but shall include no changes to the previous plan other

than those made in order to remedy those defects.

(2) If a new congressional district plan is not passed in accordance with division (B)(1) of this section and filed with the secretary of state in accordance with Section 16 of Article II of this constitution, the Ohio redistricting commission shall be reconstituted and reconvene and shall adopt a congressional district plan in accordance with the provisions of this constitution that are then valid, to be used until the next time for redistricting under this article in accordance with the provisions of this constitution that are then valid.

The commission shall adopt that plan not later than the thirtieth day after the deadline described in division (B)(1) of this section. A congressional district plan adopted under this division shall remedy any legal defects in the previous plan identified by the court but shall include no other changes to the previous plan other than those made in order to remedy those defects.

SCHEDULE

Section 1. Of Prior Laws

All laws of this state, in force on the first day of September one thousand eight hundred and fifty-one, not inconsistent with this constitution, shall continue in force, until amended, or repealed.

Section 2. The First Election of Members of General Assembly

The first election for members of the General Assembly, under this constitution, shall be held on the second Tuesday of October, one thousand eight hundred and fifty-one.

Section 3. For State Officers

The first election for governor, lieutenant governor, auditor, treasurer, and secretary of state and attorney general, shall be held on the second Tuesday of October, one thousand eight hundred and fifty-one. The persons, holding said offices on the first day of September, one thousand eight hundred and fifty-one, shall continue therein, until the second Monday of January, one thousand eight hundred and fifty-two.

Section 4. For Judges, Clerks, Etc

The first election for judges of the Supreme Court, courts of common pleas, and probate courts, and clerks of the courts of common pleas, shall be held on the second Tuesday of October, one thousand eight hundred and fifty-one, and the official term of said judges and clerks, so elected, shall commence on the second Monday of February, one thousand eight hundred and fifty-two. Judges and clerks of the courts of common pleas and Supreme Court, in office on the first day of September, one thousand eight hundred and fifty-one, shall continue in office with their present powers and duties, until the second Monday of February, one thousand eight hundred and fifty-two. No suit or proceeding, pending in any of the courts of this state, shall be affected by the adoption of this constitution.

Section 5. Officers to Continue in Office until the Expiration of Their Terms

The register and receiver of the land office, directors of the penitentiary, directors of the benevolent institutions of the state, the state librarian, and all other officers, not otherwise provided for in this constitution in office on the first day of September, one thousand eight hundred and fifty-one, shall continue in office, until their terms expire, respectively, unless the general assembly shall otherwise provide.

Section 6. Certain Courts

The superior and commercial courts of Cincinnati, and the superior court of Cleveland, shall remain, until otherwise provided by law, with their present powers and jurisdiction; and the judges and clerks of said courts, in office on the first day of September, one thousand eight hundred and fifty-one, shall continue in office, until the expiration of their terms of office, respectively, or, until otherwise provided by law; but neither of said courts shall continue after the second Monday of February, one thousand eight hundred and fifty-three; and no suits shall be commenced in said two first mentioned courts, after the second Monday of February, one thousand eight hundred and fifty-two, nor in said last mentioned court, after the second Monday in August, one thousand eight hundred and fifty-two; and all business in either of said courts, not disposed of within the time limited for their continuance as aforesaid, shall be transferred to the court of common pleas.

Section 7. County and Township Officers

All county and township officers and justices of the peace, in office on the first day of September, one thousand eight hundred and fifty-one, shall continue in office until their terms expire, respectively.

Section 8. Vacancies

Vacancies in office, occurring after the first day of September, one thousand eight hundred and fifty-one, shall be filled, as is now prescribed by law, and until officers are elected or appointed, and qualified, under this constitution.

Section 9. When Constitution Shall Take Effect

This constitution shall take effect, on the first day of September, one thousand eight hundred and fifty-one.

Section 10. Term of Office

All officers shall continue in office, until their successors shall be chosen and qualified.

Section 11. Transfer of Suits, Supreme Court

Suits pending in the Supreme Court in bank, shall be transferred to the Supreme Court provided for in this constitution, and be proceeded in according to law.

Section 12. Transfer of Suits, District Courts

The district courts shall, in their respective counties, be the successors of the present Supreme Court; and all suits, prosecutions, judgments, records, and proceedings, pending and remaining in said Supreme Court, in the several counties of any district, shall be transferred to the respective district courts of such counties, and be proceeded in, as though no change had been made in said Supreme Court.

Section 13. Transfer of Suits, Courts of Common Pleas
The said courts of common pleas, shall be the successors of the present courts of common pleas in the several counties, except as to probate jurisdiction; and all suits, prosecutions, proceedings, records and judgments, pending or being in said

last mentioned courts, except as aforesaid, shall be transferred to the courts of common pleas created by this constitution, and proceeded in, as though the same had been therein instituted.

Section 14. Transfer of Suits, Probate Courts

The probate courts provided for in this constitution, as to all matters within the jurisdiction conferred upon said courts, shall be the successors, in the several counties, of the present courts of common pleas; and the records, files, and papers, business and proceedings, appertaining to said jurisdiction, shall be transferred to said courts of probate, and be there proceeded in, according to law.

Section 15. Judges and Clerks, How Elected, Etc

Until otherwise provided by law, elections for judges and clerks shall be held, and the poll books returned, as is provided for governor, and the abstract therefrom, certified to the secretary of state, shall be by him opened, in the presence of the governor, who shall declare the result, and issue commissions to the persons elected.

Section 16. Election Returns, When Sent

Where two or more counties are joined in a senatorial, representative, or judicial district, the returns of elections shall be sent to the county, having the largest population.

Section 17. Constitution Submitted to the Electors of the State

The foregoing constitution shall be submitted to the electors of the state, at an election to be held on the third Tuesday of June, one thousand eight hundred and fifty-one, in the several election districts of this state. The ballots at such election shall be written or printed as follows: Those in favor of the constitution, "New Constitution, Yes;" those against the constitution, "New Constitution, No." The polls at said election shall be opened

between the hours of eight and ten o'clock A.M., and closed at six o'clock P.M.; and the said election shall be conducted, and the returns thereof made and certified, to the secretary of state, as provided by law for annual elections of state and county officers. Within twenty days after such election, the secretary of state shall open the returns thereof, in the presence of the governor; and, if it shall appear that a majority of all the votes, cast at such election, are in favor of the constitution, the governor shall issue his proclamation, stating that fact, and said constitution shall be the constitution of the state of Ohio, and not otherwise.
The result of this election, excluding the returns of two counties, Defiance and Auglaize, which were not received in the twenty days specified, was as follows:

"New Constitution, Yes"..................................... 125,564

"New Constitution, No" 109,276

Majority for New Constitution........................... 16,288

Section 18. License to Traffic in Intoxicating Liquors

At the time when the votes of the electors shall be taken for the adoption or rejection of this constitution, the additional section, in the words following, to wit: "No license to traffic in intoxicating liquors shall hereafter be granted in this state; but the general assembly may, by law, provide against evils resulting therefrom," shall be separately submitted to the electors for adoption or rejection, in form following, to wit: A separate ballot may be given by every elector and deposited in a separate box. Upon the ballots given for said separate amendment shall be written or printed, or partly written and partly printed, the words: "License to sell intoxicating liquors, Yes;" and upon the ballots given against said amendment, in like manner, the words: "License to sell intoxicating liquors, No." If, at the said election, a majority of all the votes given for and against said amendment, shall contain the words: "License to sell intoxicating liquors, No," then the said amendment shall be a separate section of article fifteen of the constitution.

This election resulted:

"License to sell intoxicating liquors, No"...................... 113,237

"License to sell intoxicating liquors, Yes".....................104,255

Majority against License 8,982

Section 19. Apportionment for House of Representatives

The apportionment of the House of Representatives, during the first decennial period under this constitution, shall be as follows:

The counties of:
Adams
Allen
Athens
Auglaize
Carroll
Champaign
Clark
Clinton
Crawford
Darke
Delaware
Erie, Fayette
Gallia
Geauga
Greene
Hancock
Harrison
Hocking
Holmes
Lake
Lawrence
Logan

Madison
Marion
Meigs
Morrow
Perry
Pickaway
Pike
Preble
Sandusky
Scioto
Shelby
Union...

...shall, severally, be entitled to one representative, in each session of the decennial period.

The counties of:

Franklin
Licking
Montgomery
Stark...

...shall each be entitled to two representatives, in each session of the decennial period.

The counties of:

Ashland
Coshocton
Highland
Huron
Lorain,
Mahoning
Medina
Miami
Portage
Seneca

Summit
Warren...

...shall, severally, be entitled to one representative, in each session; and one additional representative in the fifth session of the decennial period.

The counties of:

Ashtabula
Brown
Butler
Clermont
Fairfield
Guernsey
Jefferson
Knox
Monroe
Morgan
Richland
Trumbull
Tuscarawas
Washington...

...shall severally, be entitled to one representative, in each session; and two additional representatives, one in the third, and one in the fourth session of the decennial period.

The counties of:

Belmont
Columbiana
Ross
Wayne...

...shall, severally, be entitled to one representative, in each session; and three additional representatives, one in the first, one in the second, and one in the third session of the decennial period.

The county of:

Muskingum...

...shall be entitled to two representatives, in each session; and one additional representative, in the fifth session, of the decennial period.

The county of:

Cuyahoga...

...shall be entitled to two representatives, in each session; and two additional representatives, one in the third, and one in the fourth session, of the decennial period.

The county of:

Hamilton...

...shall be entitled to seven representatives, in each session; and four additional representatives, one in the first, one in the second, one in the third, and one in the fourth session, of the decennial period.

The following counties, until they shall have acquired a sufficient population to entitle them to elect, separately, under the fourth section of the eleventh article, shall form districts in manner following, to wit:

The counties of:

Jackson and Vinton, one district
Lucas and Fulton, one district

Wyandot and Hardin, one district

Mercer and Van Wert, one district

Paulding, Defiance, and Williams, one district

Putnam and Henry, one district

Wood and Ottawa, one district...

...each of which districts shall be entitled to one representative, in every session of the decennial period.

Done in convention, at Cincinnati, the tenth day of March, in the year of our Lord, one thousand eight hundred and fifty-one, and of the independence of the United States, the seventy-fifth.

WILLIAM MEDILL, President

Attest: Wm. H. Gill, Secretary

S. J. Andrews

G. Volney Dorsey

Edward Archbold

Thos. W. Ewart

William Barbee

John Ewing

Joseph Barnett

Joseph M. Farr

David Barnet

Elias Florence

Wm. S. Bates

Robert Forbes

A. I. Bennett

H. C. Gray

John H. Blair

H. N. Gillett

Jacob Blickensderfer

John Graham

Van Brown

John L. Green

A. G. Brown

Jacob J. Greene

R. W. Cahill

Henry H. Gregg

F. Case

W. S. Groesbeck

L. Case

C. S. Hamilton

David Chambers

D. D. T. Hard

John Chany

A. Harlan

H. D. Clark

William Hawkins

George Collings

James P. Henderson

Friend Cook

Peter Hitchcock

Otway Curry

G. W. Holmes

Geo. B. Holt

R. P. Ranney

John J. Hootman

Chas. Reemelin

V. B. Horton

Adam N. Riddle

Samuel Humphreville

Edward C. Roll

John E. Hunt

Wm. Sawyer

B. B. Hunter

Sabirt Scott

Reuben Hitchcock

John Sellers

John Johnson

B. P. Smith

J. Dan Jones

George J. Smith

James B. King

John A. Smith

S. J. Kirkwood

Henry Stanbery

Thos. J. Larsh

B. Stanton

William Lawrence

Albert V. Stebbins

John Larwill

E. T. Stickney

Robert Leech

Richd. Stillwell

D. P. Leadbetter

Harman Stilger

John Lidey

James Struble

James Loudon

J. R. Swan

J. McCormick

L. Swift

H. S. Manon

James W. Taylor

Samson Mason

Norton S. Townshend

Matthew H. Mitchell

Hugh Thompson

Isaiah Morris

Joseph Thompson

Charles McCloud

Joseph Vance

Simeon Nash

Elijah Vance

S. F. Norris

Wm. M. Warren

Chas. J. Orton

Thomas A. Way

W. S. C. Otis

J. Milton Williams

Thomas Patterson

Elzey Wilson

Danl. Peck

Jas. T. Worthington

Jacob Perkins

E. B. Woodbury.

Saml. Quigley

Section 20. General schedule

The several amendments passed and submitted by this convention when adopted at the election shall take effect on the first day of January, 1913, except as otherwise specifically provided by the schedule attached to any of said amendments. All laws then in force, not inconsistent therewith shall continue in force until amended or repealed; provided that all cases pending in the courts on the first day of January, 1913, shall be heard and tried in the same manner and by the same procedure as is now authorized by law. Any provision of the amendments passed and submitted by this convention and adopted by the electors, inconsistent with, or in conflict with, any provision of the present constitution, shall be held to prevail.

Section 20a. Method of Submission

The several proposals duly passed by this convention shall be submitted to the electors as separate amendments to the constitution at a special election to be held on the third day of September, 1912. The several amendments shall be designated on the ballot by their proper article and section numbers and also by their approved descriptive titles and shall be printed on said ballot and consecutively numbered in the manner and form hereinafter set forth. The adoption of any amendment by its title shall have the effect of adopting the amendment in full as finally passed by the convention. Said special election shall be held pursuant to all provisions of law applicable thereto including special registration. Ballots shall be marked in accordance with instructions printed thereon. Challengers and witnesses shall be admitted to all polling places under such regulations as may be prescribed by the secretary of state. Within ten days after said election the boards of deputy state supervisors of elections of the several counties shall forward by mail in duplicate sealed certified abstracts of the votes cast on the several amendments, one to the secretary of state and one to the auditor of state at Columbus. Within five days thereafter such abstracts shall be opened and canvassed by the secretary of state and auditor of state in the presence of the governor who shall forthwith, by proclamation, declare the results of said election. Each amendment on which the number of affirmative votes shall exceed the number of negative votes shall become a part of the constitution.

HERBERT S. BIGELOW, President

C. B. GALBREATH, Secretary

Columbus, Ohio, June 1, 1912.

David F. Anderson

A. V. Donahey

Ernest I. Antrim

Edward W. Doty

John L. Baum

Charles O. Dunlap

Robert A. Beatty

Alexander Dunn

A. Beyer

Dennis Dwyer

Stanley E. Bowdle

Henry E. Eby

Wesley B. Brattain

J. Milton Earnhart

H. M. Brown

Henry W. Elson

Walter F. Brown

John D. Fackler

M. A. Brown

W. W. Farnsworth

William W. Campbell

Thomas S. Farrell

John R. Cassidy

S. D. Fess

M. T. Cody

Thos. G. FitzSimons

Bernard Y. Collett

James M. Fluke

Geo. H. Colton

Henry C. Fox

Henry F. Cordes

Aaron Hahn

Henry M. Crites

Wm. P. Halenkamp

Robert Crosser

James W. Halfhill

David Cunningham

James W. Harbarger

William C. Davio

Wm. S. Harris

Joe DeFrees

Geo. W. Harris

Otto M. Harter

W. E. Partington

Isaac Harter

Hiram D. Peck

Robert Henderson

Edward A. Peters

John C. Hoffman

Geo. W. Pettit

Charles D. Holtz

David Pierce

Samuel A. Hoskins

T. D. Price

Frank G. Hursh

A. Ross Read

Edward W. Johnson

Horace G. Redington

Solomon Johnson

Jno. H. Riley

Humphrey Jones

Wm. M. Rockel

J. W. Kehoe

John Roehm

Henry C. Keller

John C. Rorick

Frank H. Kerr

Stanley Shaffer

Wm. B. Kilpatrick

Eli D. Shaw

E. B. King

H. K. Smith

G. W. Knight

Starbuck Smith

John F. Kramer

J. C. Solether

Lawrence P. Kunkle

Franklin J. Stalter

Frank P. Lambert

M. Stamm

E. L. Lampson

W. B. Stevens

Fred G. Leete

O. H. Stewart

Daniel E. Leslie

Stephen S. Stillwell

Robert B. Longstreth

William Worth Stokes

Chris Ludey

Frank Taggart

Fletcher D. Malin

James C. Tallman

Frank M. Marriott

J. W. Tannehill

Allen M. Marshall

Percey Tetlow

N.E. Matthews

Harry D. Thomas

Roscoe J. Mauck

John Ulmer

R. G. McClelland

Edwin T. Wagner

Geo. W. Miller

Wilmer R. Walker

Frank P. Miller

Harvey Watson

Wm. Miller

Benj. F. Weybrecht

Illion E. Moore

John W. Winn

Caleb H. Norris

Frank C. Wise

David J. Nye

F. W. Woods

J. A. Okey

Wm. Worthington

Section 21. Schedule to Article 2 Sections 1, 1a, 1b, 1c, 1d, 1e, 1f, and 1g

The foregoing amendment, if adopted by the electors shall take effect on October 1, 1912.

Section 22. Schedule to Article 4 Sections 1, 2, 3, 6, 7, 12, and 15

If the foregoing amendment shall be adopted by the electors, the judges of the courts of common pleas in office, or elected thereto prior to January first, 1913, shall hold their offices for the term for which they were elected and the additional judges provided for herein, shall be elected at the general election in the year 1914; each county shall continue as a part of its existing common pleas district and sub-division thereof, until one resident judge of the court of common pleas is elected and qualified therein.

Section 23. Schedule to Article 6 Sections 3 and 4

If the foregoing amendment be adopted by the electors it shall take effect ad become part of the constitution on the second Monday of July, 1913.

Section 24. Schedule to Article 18 Sections 1-14

If the foregoing amendment to the constitution be adopted by the electors and become a part of the constitution, it shall take effect on November 15th, 1912.

Section 25. Schedule to Article 15 Section 9

If the proposed amendment be adopted, it shall become section 9 of Article XV of the constitution, and it shall take effect on the 27th day of May of the year following the date of the election at which it is adopted, at which time original sections 9 and 9a of Article XV of the constitution and all statutes inconsistent with the foregoing amendment shall be repealed.

Section 26. Schedule to Article 12 Sections 2 and 3

If the votes for the proposal shall exceed those against it, the amendment shall go into effect January 1, 1931, and original sections 2 and 3 of article XII of the constitution of the state of Ohio shall be repealed and annulled; but all levies for interest and sinking fund or retirement of bonds issued, or authorized prior to said date which are not subject to the statutory limitation of fifteen mills on the aggregate rate of taxation then in force, and all tax levies provided for by the conservancy act of Ohio and the sanitary district act of Ohio, as said laws are in force on said date, for the purposes of conservancy districts and sanitary districts organized prior to said date, and all tax levies for other purposes authorized by the General Assembly prior to said date or by vote of the electors of any political subdivision of the state, pursuant to laws in force on said date, to be made outside said statutory limitation for and during a period of years extending beyond said date, to be made outside said statutory limitation for and during a period of years extending beyond said date, or provided for by the charter of a municipal corporation pursuant to laws in force on said date, shall not be subject to the limitation of fifteen mills established by said amendment; and levies for interest and sinking fund or retirement of bonds issued or authorized prior to said date, shall be outside of said limitation to the extent required to equalize any reduction in the amount of taxable property available for such levies, or in the rate imposed upon such property, effected by laws thereafter passed.

Section 27. Schedule to Article 12 Sections 2 and 3

If the votes for the proposal shall exceed those against it, the amendment shall go into effect January 1, 1931, and original sections 2 and 3 of article XII of the constitution of the state of Ohio shall be repealed and annulled; but all levies for interest and sinking fund or retirement of bonds issued, or authorized prior to said date which are not subject to the statutory limitation of fifteen mills on the aggregate rate of taxation then in force, and all tax levies provided for by the conservancy act of Ohio and the sanitary district act of Ohio, as said laws are in force on said date, for the purposes of conservancy districts and sanitary districts organized prior to said date, and all tax levies for other purposes authorized by the General assembly prior to said date or by vote of the electors of any political subdivision of the state, pursuant to laws in force on said date, to be made outside said statutory limitation for and during a period of years extending beyond said date, or provided for by the charter of a municipal corporation pursuant to laws in force on said date, shall not be subject to the limitation of fifteen mills established by said amendment; and levies for interest and sinking fund or retirement of bonds issued or authorized prior to said date, shall be outside of said limitation of the extent required to equalize any reduction in the amount of taxable property available for such levies, or in the rate by laws thereafter passed.

Section 28. Schedule to Article 12 Section 2

If the votes for the proposal shall exceed those against it, the amendment shall go into effect January 1, 1934, and existing Section 2 of Article XII of the Constitution of the state of Ohio shall be repealed and annulled, but the following exuberated levies shall not be subject to the limitation of one per cent established by such amendment: (1) All levies for interest and sinking fund or retirement of bonds issued or authorized prior to said date which are not subject to the present limitation of one and one-half per cent imposed by Section 2 of Article XII and the schedule thereto as approved by the electors of the state on November 5, 1929; (2) All tax levies provided for by the conservancy act of Ohio or the sanitary district act of Ohio, as said laws are in force on January 1, 1934, for the purpose of conservancy districts and sanitary districts organized prior to said date; (3) All tax levies authorized prior to said date by vote of the electors of any political subdivision of the state, pursuant to laws in force at the time of such vote, to be made for or during a period of years extending beyond January 1, 1934, which levies are outside of the present limitation of one and one-half per cent imposed by Section 2 of Article XII ad the schedule thereto as approved on November 5, 1929; and (4) All tax levies provided for by the charter of a municipal corporation pursuant to law and which were authorized prior to January 1, 1934, and are not subject to the present limitation of one and one-half per cent imposed by said section and schedule as approved on November 5, 1929.

Section 29. Schedule to Article 6 Section 4

If the vote for the proposal shall exceed those against it, the foregoing shall take immediate effect and existing section 4 of article VI of the constitution shall be repealed and annulled. The superintendent of public instruction, in office when the foregoing amendment takes effect, shall continue therein until the superintendent of public institution for whom provision is made under the foregoing amendment shall have been appointed and shall have qualified.

Section 30. Schedule to Article 4 Sections 1-14 and Article 11 Sections 12 and 13

If adopted by a majority of the electors voting on this amendment, the amendment except paragraph (b) of the Schedule shall take effect January 10, 1970, and existing sections 1 and 2, and sections 3, 4, 6, 7, 8, 10, 12, and 14 of Article IV of the Constitution of Ohio shall be repealed from such effective date. Paragraph (b) of the Schedule and the repeal of sections 12 and 13 of Article XI adopted in 1851, shall become effective immediately upon the adoption of this amendment by the electors of this state. Upon the effective date of this amendment:

(A) Provision shall be made by law for the disposition of all pending cases in accordance with the procedural law in effect at the time of the effective date of this amendment.

(B) In accordance with the provisions of this article, the General Assembly shall enact such laws and the Supreme Court shall promulgate such rules as will give effect to the provisions herein.

(C) All laws and rules of court in existence upon the effective date of this amendment shall continue in effect until superseded or changed in the manner authorized by this amendment.

(D) All judges of the probate courts shall become judges of the courts of common pleas.

(E) Any judge who is holding office on December 31, 1969, and who would be eligible for re-election in 1970 for a term beginning in 1971 except for his age and the provisions of division (C) of Section 6, Article IV, shall be eligible nevertheless to be re-elected in 1970 for one additional term as judge of the same court.

Section 31. Schedule to Article 3 Sections 1b and 16

Section 1b of Article III authorizing the governor to assign duties in the executive department to the lieutenant governor and the repeal of section 16 of Article III shall not take effect until the second Monday in January, 1979.

Section 32. Schedule to Article 3 Section 22

If, on the effective date of this amendment, section number 16 is already assigned to a section of Article III of the Constitution of Ohio, the secretary of state shall assign section number22 to the section in Article III that would be numbered section 16 by this amendment, and such number shall be the official number of such section and shall be so published in any publication of the constitution and shall be cited and referred to by such number.

Section 33. Schedule to Article 12 Section 9

If, on the effective date of this amendment, section number 6 is already assigned to a section in Article XII that would be amended by this amendment to include a renumbering of the section from section 9 to section 6, and such number shall be the official number of such section and shall be so published in any publication of the constitution and shall be cited and referred to by such number.

www.ingramcontent.com/pod-product-compliance
Lightning Source LLC
Chambersburg PA
CBHW052310220526
45472CB00001B/53